MW00879913

AFTER

THE STORY OF HOW I'VE TURNED

THEY

MY SEXUAL TRAUMA INTO A

TOUCHED

GLORIOUS TRIUMPH

ME

SHARONA DRAKE
FOREWORD BY ADRIAN DAVIS

SHARONA DRAKE
After They Touched Me
The Story Of How I've Turned My Sexual Trauma Into A Glorious Triumph

Printed in the United States of America
ISBN-13: 978-1722855147
ISBN-10: 1722855142

www.sharonadrake.com

AFTER

THE STORY OF HOW I'VE TURNED

THEY

MY SEXUAL TRAUMA INTO A

TOUCHED

GLORIOUS TRIUMPH

ME

SHARONA DRAKE
FOREWORD BY ADRIAN DAVIS

DEDICATION

This book is dedicated to every survivor of sexual trauma. This is for you… that you may move from a survivor to a healer. I love you. You are more than enough, but never too much. God's purpose for your life hasn't been readjusted based on your past.

EVERYTHING IS EASY FOR JESUS!

CONTENTS

ACKNOWLEDGEMENTS

Mom, thank you for your resilience.

Dad, thank you for believing that I heard from God when I decided to write this.

Jasmine, Khea, and Isa, thank you for walking with me as I "became."

Tosha, Anna, and Tanya, thank you for being my friends.

Pastor Edsel Cadet, Charles, Mike Trout, Ndubuisi, and John, thank you for being generals in my life.

Apostles Matthew & Kamilah Stevenson, thank you for establishing All Nations Worship Assembly for people like me and for helping to bring my future into the now.

Pastor Adrian "AD" Davis, your boldness, sincerity, and transparency have changed my life and the lives of many. You're the type of world changer I will always believe in. Thank you for your yes.

And to **my team, the Hit Squad,** I love you all. You make the future feasible. Let's conquer together.

FOREWORD

I have had the privilege of knowing Sharona Drake for almost a decade now. Even still, I find it amazing how you can know someone for such a length of time but not realize how connected your personal stories are until specific details are divulged. *After They Touched Me* provides insight into Sharona's backstory that not only gave me a raw look into who she is but also allowed me to reflect on my personal journey of pursuing triumph after experiencing sexual trauma. Reading this book, I became convinced that Sharona relived some tough and trying times to offer us a transparent, real, and raw look into the plight of her sexual trauma and her road to healing. It is to the benefit of many people like me that she took such an authentic risk.

As someone who was also molested, I connected with *After They Touched Me* on a myriad of levels, but the "Awareness" section of the book resonated with me the most. At one point in my life, the effects of my abuse branched out into almost every area of my life and heart, but it still took me a while to come to my own awareness about it all. So when I read about Sharona's process of identifying and confronting her difficulties with connecting with others, settling in romantic relationships, submitting to authority, and receiving authentic love, I thoroughly understood her mindset.

In a world where men and women are barely mentally, spiritually, and emotionally surviving following their sexual trauma, *After They Touched Me* is needed on so many levels. It is especially for those of us who secretly battled with, or are currently fighting with telling our close loved ones about our abuse. And it is even for those of us just coming into our own realities about our past experiences and any current unhealthy coping habits. The content and spirit of openness in this book is needed so that many of us can break into new places of freedom.

This book does not exist for people to read so that they can have another excuse to remain in isolation or under the dictatorship of their past. It is a tool written so that they can look at themselves and, much like the Chapter 8 states, choose to become "100 % responsible, 100% of the time."

After They Touched Me allows us to follow the journey of someone who decided that she would take authority of her own healing process instead of waiting for wholeness to just happen to her on its own. Sharona's story is an encouragement to us to become owners of our own mental and emotional health, and I personally can attest to the fact that taking full responsibility for the state of my life was a primary key to my therapeutic process. I'm confident that if readers apply the principles of personal ownership presented in this book, it will be a major key in helping them to heal as well.

I expect that there will be many grateful readers of *After They Touched Me* who will gain broader perspectives on how to untangle and combat the effects of sexual trauma and still thrive. Do yourself a favor and start your journey of finding triumph after trauma by reading this book and not looking back until you've completed it!

I just have four words for you: Enjoy your new freedom!

Adrian D. Davis
Pastor, Leader, Author, and Designer
2018

INTRODUCTION

My childhood was filled with a lot of fantastic memories: my mom teaching me how to read as a toddler, playing in the park with my dad in Fort Bragg, NC, creating an alternate universe with my Barbies, and so much more. Although I grew up in a dangerous neighborhood, my home was most certainly filled with laughter and joy. However, there were other memories as well—some vivid, early childhood memories that haunted me for decades. Before I could write my name, before I stopped peeing in the bed… I was sexually traumatized.

One of my earliest sexual encounters involved being taken into the closet by an older boy. He told me to take off my shirt and kiss him in places no little girl needed to kiss anyone. Then there was the boy who dry humped me, rubbing his genitals on me in front of a small group of older kids. They laughed and cheered us on, all while threatening me by saying we wouldn't be friends unless I let him do what they wanted him to do to my body. I was just five or six years old then. Before I turned eight years old, girls from church and other trusted places introduced me to orgies.

In recent years, through counseling, I've accepted the fact that some of the recurring dreams that I've had since I was a child weren't dreams at all. They were and always will be memories. I've realized that an older man who was trusted to watch me as a child was actually grooming me sexually. He taught me that moaning when a man, especially one you love, touched you was a sign of respect and appreciation, and I believed everything he taught me.

I knew about sex before I could part my hair straight (well, I still can't do that, but you get the point). While I was still wearing pigtails and was memorizing John 3:16 and Phil 4:13, I was abused by those within the church. In those early years, scriptures, shouting, and sexual sin went hand in hand. The same things I'm celebrated for–public speaking, singing, writing, mentoring, having a love for scripture, leading—were all instilled in me while I was learning about oral sex. I was groomed and programmed to enjoy sinful sexual expression while simultaneously being taught about righteousness.

My mom was so adamant that I'd have a godly upbringing. But I also had substitute teachers. They taught me to keep secrets, cover my emotions, touch men and women in certain ways to make them feel good, moan and show appreciation if I wanted friends, and to tell my mind and body to enjoy the sordid beauty of it all. And, just like everything else I'm celebrated for, I mastered almost everything

I was taught by those substitute teachers.

I heard the holiness talks early, sometimes by the same ones who were living double lives and touching me. I understood that God hated fornication and adultery and all kinds of sin. I knew that the pure in heart shall see God. But sometimes, just sometimes, I wished that people could take a few steps in my shoes to consider what it might've been like to be introduced to sex before the consequences of lust were even a part of my understanding.

And so I've had my struggles. I battled because I've always loved God and have wanted to honor Him and myself, but undoing this training has been the most ferocious fight of my life. I struggled for years because, when I met with mentors, they equated my love for God to my outward sexual purity only. Oftentimes they asked about my sex life more than they inquired about the roots of my issues and how they could provide support in helping me heal. Many of my mentors and leaders didn't understand that, while setting up boundaries enabled me not to commit certain outward acts, leaving the broader issues of my heart untouched left me just as dirty and broken as when I was giving into the sexual desires physically. My love for God had been ranked by how often I'd fallen in a year as opposed to how much progress I'd made in unraveling the tangled mess of my heart and surrendering and trusting God with the process of developing new habits. For a while, the message I heard was if I "really loved God," then I would just overcome sexual sin, preferably instantly or within a few months, and that if I "really had the Spirit of God," I wouldn't fall anymore.

I understood the good intentions of many who sent me one-sided messages, but I often ended up confused. On the one hand, I was told that I wasn't saved by works, but on the other hand, it seemed that my works were used to determine my state of salvation. It was hard for me to accept that I could love God and still have things to work on. I wondered if sanctification really was a process of becoming more like Christ or a one-time deliverance event. I wondered if there was any hope for me at all. I mean, faith without works is dead, right? *Why couldn't I just seem to get my works together?!*

Oh, how I thank God for greater revelation! I am so grateful that He is enough and that He sees our journeys and celebrates the sanctification taking place through His Spirit. I am humbled by the fact that He shows us favor and gives us insight even though He sees our mess… that He has actually provided a way for us to have our stains cleaned and to use our process to bless others.

And that's what this book is about… finding victory in the process.

What to Expect

This book is not a "how to" guide. In fact, the steps of my healing and wholeness aren't even linear. It's more of a recurring cycle I go through in higher levels at each new season of life. As I mature during each phase of life and follow the principles I present to you in *After They Touched Me* (ATTM), I learn more about myself, recognize deeper roots of behavior patterns, and experience more significant victories.

The steps that I've gone through to find my triumph after sexual trauma are meant to inspire you to find (possibly long lost) hope in establishing your own path to freedom and embracing your individual process towards wholeness. In this book, I present ideas that I hope will help you to dream again, to accept that you are not bound to your sexual abuse, and to walk in the fact that your life need not be defined by what others have done to you or what you have given yourself over to.

You are still worthy of the promises and the purpose that you were created to live out. You may have experienced a lot of crap in your life, but manure has always been an excellent fertilizer for plants to grow! The seed deposited in our lives still contains our destiny, and we do not have to forfeit the fruit of abundant life if we don't want to.

After years of immense struggle in various areas, I can happily say that God has given me major inward and outward victories. I've learned to establish healthy opposite and same-sex friendships; I have learned to love my body without objectifying it; I am growing in maintaining boundaries that declare my worth, and I am even walking in a higher level of purity than I ever have.

I've also learned that I had victory even when my mentors and friends couldn't see it, even when I failed to see that God was working on my roots when I had nothing visible for others to celebrate. I'm also fully aware that outward victories don't negate the fact that I still have a long way to go in my walk with wholeness and purity because, well, it is a process. I've just gotten much farther than I ever imagined at one point, and for that I am grateful.

My good friend Tanya once encouraged me by saying, *"If God could say that Day Three of creation was 'good,' even though it wasn't complete, then I can definitely say that I'm in a good place too, even while still being perfected."* And so, I'm learning to keep an open ear to God so I can be sober-minded about what "day" I'm on with Him and if He is calling my current state "good," even if we both know that it is not complete.

I've written this book to help you and others like you to dig deep, take control of your personal narrative, set and reach new goals, and celebrate the victories of where you are today. Each day has troubles, challenges, and deep self-revelations of its own, but each day also brings new grace, new mercies, and new opportunities to win!

You *can* experience triumph even after your sexual trauma! Every bitter lemon has the potential to become a part of the sweetest, thirst-quenching lemonade. I'm here to help you make it sweet!

Let's pray.

Dear Heavenly Father,

Thank You for never giving up on us. Sometimes it has been hard to see how a just God could allow bad things to happen to us, but we are taking the chance to trust your goodness again. We are grateful that the abuse had boundaries and that You blocked our sexual trauma from becoming worse than what it has been. We are still alive!

And now, we choose to hope for our future. We decide to take control of our lives and to pursue triumph in the face of our trauma. We choose to cry, to war, to laugh, to question, to answer, to love, and to journey.

Be with every reader and allow the words of this book to penetrate the hearts of many generations of wounded Believers and Unbelievers alike. We're willing to try again, and we believe that You can help us. Yet even still, help our unbelief.

Amen.

Exposure

> *"Cry Jay Z, we know the pain is real. But you can't heal what you never reveal."*
>
> *- Jay-Z*

THE STORY OF HOW I'VE TURNED MY SEXUAL TRAUMA INTO A GLORIOUS TRIUMPH

# 1 ONE IN EIGHT

"There are wounds that never show on the body that are deeper and more hurtful than anything that bleeds."
- Laurell K. Hamilton

Some years ago, I sat in my college psychology class as my professor mentioned that one in eight people had been victims of sexual assault in their lifetime (the statistics have since narrowed). My professor then went on to list off the effects of such trauma on mental and emotional development. I grievously scanned the class, filled with young men and women who I had been studying with for over two years, trying to figure out which of them were the survivors dealing with the list of seemingly hopeless effects being presented.

I remember inspecting all of their faces, wondering how I had known them all for so long and yet never discussed this topic with any of them. I remember the sorrow that perforated my heart as I imagined how those classmates of mine must have felt about discussing sexual abuse at that moment, how heavy the burden must have been for them to carry the effects of their experiences day to day. I ached for them as I tried to figure out how I'd deal with something so jarring, unexpected, and life-altering.

On another honest note, I was also nosey and wanted to grab some popcorn, sip some tea, and hear a good "Lifetime story" (you know how it is sometimes). But then I realized that the pain the people in that class must've felt wasn't a movie to them. It was their lives.

I prayed for the unknown survivors, deciding to stand in the gap and intercede for them, more than willing to walk out the healing process with anyone if they would've chosen to share. I prayed and pondered... that was until childhood flashbacks of molestation began beating my brain, each blink of my eye bringing about another sad revelation.

Could it really be true? I realized that I was the one I was looking for and petitioning God for. I, in fact, was one in eight.

How did I miss this glaring fact about my own life?!

Yes, I had always had some memories of early childhood sexual experiences, even as early as three years old, but somehow, I had disconnected from the experiences so much that I never identified them as abuse.

Maybe it was the fact that I had become so accustomed to certain encounters that a part of me had normalized, and even invited, the abuse after some time. Maybe it was because the last time I allowed myself to fully feel the pain of my past, I wanted to kill myself. That was in eighth grade.

Maybe it was because the adults in my life who knew about some of the things that happened to me continued to live their own lives with some sense of normalcy. Maybe it was simply because I had consented to the rape culture I was raised in, telling myself what happened wasn't *that* bad since I wasn't actually raped, made good grades in school, "knew God," and had become a leader within my small community. *Shoot!* Maybe it was because I loved good foreplay and sex from time to time (because seriously, who doesn't?!) and didn't know how to separate abuse from desire.

Whatever the reason, it was at that moment, as our class reviewed the list of the effects of sexual trauma on social-emotional development, that I could see myself for the first time. As I went through my life's Rolodex of relationships, academic achievements, and behavior patterns, I found a common thread: brokenness. And the bigger problem I saw was that, the more the years had gone by, the deeper and longer the cracks in my foundation had gotten as I ignored the overwhelmingly large and stinky elephants in the inner rooms of my heart and mind.

The epiphany of that day reminds me of a lesson I once taught a mentee of mine. One night there was a rather large, scary-looking spider on the back of her vehicle, creating the most intricate web with lightning speed. Because my mentee was afraid of spiders and had already endured a long day, she determined that she would deal with it all the next morning. That night, I looked her in the eyes and presented her with her options and consequences in a new light.

Her first option was that she could leave the spider overnight and choose to take care of it in the morning. The possible consequences included that the web that the spider was building would be more extensive by the time she got to her car in the morning and that there was no telling what insects would be caught and killed in the web overnight. I also let her know that although the spider was visible that night, there was no promise that the spider would be in the same position the next day. She could experience more fear the following day, not knowing where the spider was located, but seeing evidence of its presence wrapped around her vehicle.

Her other option was that she could take care of the spider and its web that evening. The potential consequences of this option would include her having to fight through her fatigue and face an overwhelming fear of hers. But she could rest well knowing she was victorious and that she would be fully prepared to make it to her first destination the next day without experiencing any delay. She could eradicate any future fears by dealing with her current issue. As a result of this conversation, my mentee decided to kill the spider that night. She chose to destroy it and dismantle the webs even though she was still afraid.

I continue to learn from that night.

Just like her, I decided that day in class that it was time to enter into the process of untangling an ugly web of trauma that unwelcomed abusers had initiated in my heart and mind. It was time to uproot negativity, clear out the weeds and stones in the soil of what had become Sharona, and to plant seeds that would blossom into a flourishing garden of wholeness and peace.

To See Or Not To See

"Patience doesn't mean making a pact with the devil of denial, ignoring our emotions and aspirations. It means being wholeheartedly engaged in the process that's unfolding, rather than ripping open a budding flower or demanding a caterpillar hurry up and get that chrysalis stage over with."
- Sharon Salzberg

Believe it or not, accepting that I had been abused was tough for me. I don't know if it was because most of my childhood sexual abuse had been at the hands of older teenagers or just because I thought I was too strong of a woman to have ever been taken advantage of, but either way, it was difficult. I struggled with the thought of saying that any minor or adult in their twenties could be the source of abuse, that only an older adult could molest a child. I had to deal with the fact that maybe the twenty-something-year-old men I thought I was in a relationship with at twelve and thirteen were taking advantage of me while I was busy believing that our love was real because I was "mature for my age."

There were so many thoughts to juggle.

Did I ask to be touched inappropriately by the way I behaved? I never said "no," so was I really rejecting advances? Did I do something to make older girls think that they could touch me and make me participate in their orgies at such a young age? Did that mean that I was bisexual?

It just seemed so much easier to ignore everything that happened, cling to religiosity, and make a vow of purity before God than to actually try to answer the questions. After all, I was a new creature in Christ, right (2 Corinthians 5:17)? The Bible *did* tell me to press forward and to forget the things that were behind me (Philippians 3:14). I wondered if I could become "Christian enough" to just get over it all. I mean, I wasn't raped so it couldn't have been that bad, right?

The interesting thing about the past is that, when you fail to deal with it, it remains a part of your present and tries to dictate your future. It is a weed, and its goal is to strangle all of the flourishing flowers around it.

As many good seeds that had been planted in my life's garden— grades that led to a scholarship, leadership opportunities in my church and community, artistic abilities, life skills from my parents, etc.—I noticed unhealthy patterns in my life. I was only reaching certain heights in my performance before I began to choke. I continued to have sex a lot even though I had committed to myself time and time again to have higher standards for my body. I found myself hiding behind my gifts, sexuality, spirituality, intellect, and anything else that would keep anyone from getting to know me. And I'd often be disappointed when people left me or misunderstood me (although I didn't give them much to work with).

Of course, I seemed strong and independent on the outside, but my lack of self-control in the private, meaningful areas of my heart showed me how dependent I actually was to feeding the beast my abuse had created. I was codependent in my need for affirmation through sex, love from men, accomplishments, and so much more.

To be honest, when I realized how deeply troubling things actually were, I often would decide to give up trying to be who I felt God was calling me to be. *Shoot!* Forget who God was calling me to be. I was failing at who I even wanted to be!

I had tried to "do right" by God and man, but I kept falling short. I thought maybe freedom just wasn't for me. Maybe if I got married to an amazing man and we were able to have sex freely, I'd be ok. Or maybe freedom would be for my future kids or their children. Or maybe freedom was an illusion created by "the Man" to keep me a slave to moral standards that God didn't even care about. Baby, I was *all* mixed up, hear?

I would also find myself wondering what freedom was anyway. I knew what people had *told* me freedom was, but what did that look like for Sharona? I had never thought about that before, and that sent me on my own personal journey to figure out what I truly wanted out of life.

2 CHOOSING FREEDOM

"The secret to happiness is freedom...
And the secret to freedom is courage."
- Thucydides

One of the most powerful things that I did at the genesis of my journey was to define what freedom and success would look like for me at that time. I had given so much of my basic control to my past, my sexual appetite, my abusers, and "Christian standards," that I had never sat down, looked at my life, and thought about what I actually wanted for myself and what God was genuinely saying about my purpose.

At first, defining my freedom seemed exciting, you know? I figured that I would get to use my imagination to paint a picture of the good things that I wanted, write them down, and then somehow achieve them. However, I soon realized the strength of the stronghold that held on to my mind.

You see, as soon as I decided to dream, I was reminded of my nightmares. I heard the voices of my past telling me that I had participated in too much sex to think that any man would want me and that being promiscuous (or sexually "liberated") was ingrained in me. The voices told me that if I decided to take my walls down to trust and love people again that I'd end up hurt like I was before, wanting to commit suicide again.

"Even the Liberty Bell has a crack in it. Even it is broken. What makes you think that you can even dream of being whole?!" The past rang in my ear louder than I had ever noticed.

At the same time those voices were speaking to me, I heard the sound of freedom beckoning me to dream again. I listened to my future calling me into greatness, hope telling me that I had a choice to slingshot the Cornerstone of Christ at the giants of my past. The verses that I had memorized in church while being abused began to muzzle the voices of darkness and became more than black words on white paper.

What if I could actually do all things through Christ who strengthens me? What if God really could make my scarlet sins as white as snow, and I could hold my head up despite my past and present struggles? What if someone could love me for who I was and not just how I could please them? What if I was already loved?

And what if I hadn't even seen the real potential of how powerful I was created to be?

I had a decision to make about the voice that I'd listen to. It would be easier, to some extent, to just live life the way I had known or to even lower the bar of what I would dream my life to be. On the other hand, I considered that the possibilities of hope were endless, and the little girl who was the songwriter and playwright, the one who imagined being "the next Oprah" and created worlds with her Barbies, may still be able to dream and even play a role in creating her own reality.

I knew what continuing life the way I had known it would lead to. I had seen friends and family members who carried the burden of sexual abuse their entire lives. From my own experience, I knew I could accomplish much externally and be "successful" by the world's standards. However, I questioned if many of the people I knew who had survived abuse would actually call themselves successful internally. I knew I couldn't say that about myself. I wondered if their internal brokenness was the cause of their low standards with friends and at the root of their romantic issues and lack of ability to truly connect with God and others. However, I also wondered if attempting to deal with my sexual trauma head-on could actually lead to personal triumph.

I was interested in discovering if freedom was on the other side of my fear and I was too much of a risk taker to choose anything other than the road less traveled.

Defining My Success

"Success is not final; failure is not fatal: It is the courage to continue that counts."- Winston S. Churchill

After choosing the path of freedom, I had to move forward with silencing the voices of my past. For me, that meant I had to have the audacity to be more authentic than I had ever been. That was my first definition of success: being honest and open with myself and others.

Because of my trust and insecurity issues, I couldn't yet choose one person to be wholly uninhibited with (and if I'm being real, I've still caught myself struggling with that now), so I created a "safety net." I decided that I'd be forthright about everything I was dealing with, but I'd split up what parts of myself I'd share with certain people (you know, so no one person could hurt me too bad).

For the first time, I chose to talk to people about my sexual abuse and experiences as a child. At first, I would only tell bits and pieces, but at least I was talking, and after a while, sharing became less and less arduous. I realized that people were more understanding than I thought they would be and that, in many cases, I wasn't alone. I was also optimistic about advancing in my process because the more I shared, the more I was living a successful life, according to the goal I had defined.

As I progressed in that season, I also began to share more details about my real-time sexual exploits with my best friend, Jasmine. I would tell her about who I was trying to get in bed (which I now know was total manipulation in an effort to feel a sense of control) or whose man I was messing around with (which was my way of proving to myself that I was as pretty or valuable as another woman) or whatever else I shouldn't have been doing (which was a whole lot). She was a steady, wise ear that didn't judge me, but she was definitely an expert at asking me high-level questions about my true motives and how they matched up to the public commitments I made to God and myself. Her approach worked for me, so I continued to share with her because although I needed a safe space to be genuine and flawed, I also still yearned for a certain level of accountability. I was wild back then, and I'm sure Jasmine remembers stories that would go viral if told today. Lord knows I'm glad that she was, and continues to be, an intercessor and vault of information. Your girl was out there twirling and twerking on the menfolk back in the day, and everyone needs to forget about that, *ok*?! *(Lawd, please be a memory eraser to all the people who saw things that they shouldn't have!)*

The most important person that I began to be honest with, however, was God. For the first time, I was free enough to share my deepest thoughts with Him about who I was and how my trauma made me feel. I asked Him questions, told Him when I was angry with Him, shared my doubts and fears, and learned to quit trying to be something I wasn't for Him. To be more accurate, in that season, I learned to stop trying almost altogether. "Trying" had always led to failure, which led to me feeling condemned and hopeless, which led to me shutting someone out of my life or bringing someone into my bed. Instead, I told God that if He wanted me, He'd have to fix me. I never stopped talking to Him, and I didn't shut down on Him, but I did tell Him that if He wanted me to be whole, then He'd have to do the work.

My "quitting approach" appeared to be illogical, but it was imperative for me to surrender my efforts in that season. For so long I worked to please God and people but didn't have the strength to live up to their standards. On my journey, I consistently ran into Believers who implied that I was a hypocrite because I struggled with sins that they thought I should have conquered at that time. Their words suggested that I didn't really love God. It hurt to hear their assessments of me and to feel that I failed so often and for so long. However, I began to let go of trying to work for my own righteousness. Instead, I focused on getting to know God and becoming acquainted with my own identity. It was then that I realized my Divine Daddy wasn't threatened or judgmental about the time my course of healing was taking. In fact, He seemed to embrace my process. I wondered if maybe it was because He lived outside of time and could see my true future more than any of us could. It also seemed like God preferred to take His time with me in certain areas. I finally began to become settled with allowing His Spirit to sanctify me in His time.

Looking back, I now honestly believe 2 Peter 3:9, where it says that *"the Lord isn't being slow about his promise, as some people think, but that He is being patient for our sake."* His faith in me made my love for Him grow. Even though my end goals were much more significant than just being honest, God's patience with me allowed me to be satisfied in Him and hopeful for the future. The work wasn't complete, but for that season, I was good.

I now know that I'll never be more invested in my future than Jesus is. God was with me as I took the little steps towards living a truthful life, and that gave me grace for the struggles that were ahead of me. Every mini victory became a building block of what would later become the monument of my triumphant history with God. He was not only helping me to define my success, but He was allowing me to see that He had already won my battles on the cross. I was merely receiving training in how to live out what was already given to me as a gift. My restoration was one of the spoils conquered in a war that Jesus won on His own.

Awareness

"Until you make the unconscious conscious, it will direct your life and you will call it fate."

-C.G. Jung

3

ASKING QUESTIONS

"Self awareness is the ability to take an honest look at your life without any attachment to it being right or wrong, good or bad."
- Debbie Ford

It is common for people to still deal with the effects of their childhood sexual trauma well into their adulthood,. Many adult survivors harbor guilt, shame, and blame; struggle with intimacy and relationships; and have low self-esteem as well. We also can have severe anxiety, PTSD, feelings of powerlessness, addictive behavior, sleep disturbances, eating problems, and so much more (rainn.org). As I began to face the facts about my molestation, I had to truly dig deep to find the ways that my past had contributed to my present. I decided that I needed to locate and address the roots of disorder in my life.

I realized that my default desire was to believe that nothing was wrong with me and that any signs of dysfunction were a result of me going through natural phases that would fix themselves on their own over time. I mean, I had all of the Black Girl Magic in the world so I couldn't actually have issues, right? *attempts to flip stiff natural afro*

Through my lens of denial, I looked at my past relationships, and I could clearly see why things didn't work out because of the *other* person's flaws. Only if I squinted really, really, really hard, could I partially see the little tiny role that I played in romantic relationships not working out. Well! It was time to take those tainted lenses off and put on those old 1980s, thick, plastic bifocal lenses that my mama used to wear and be real with myself. I needed some healing.

I had to be willing to ask and answer the hard questions.

One of the most helpful questions I learned to ask as I continued to heal was, "What's wrong with me?" Over time I learned not to ask that question in a self-deprecating, victimizing way, but rather with a pure, inquisitive heart that was serious about obtaining answers. Reflecting upon my relationships, I realized that I had significant difficulty with connecting with other young women, settling with men, submitting to authority, receiving love, and so much more.

When it came to women, it wasn't that I struggled with jealousy or thought that all women came with drama as many young ladies believed. I just didn't know how to connect with them even when

I wanted one to be my friend. There was some wall I put up that kept me at a distance. I didn't feel like one of "them." I loved playing with Barbies, but other than that, I was into sports, climbing fences, boxing, and the like... very few "dainty" things. I was intimidated by well-kept, pretty women who seemed to have all of their feminine ducks in a row.

As far as my male friends were concerned, I was often "one of the boys" to them. As I reflect back, one of my middle school friends was the perfect example of my male friendships. Me and John (and y'all know that was not his actual Wakanda-sounding name, but I have to play it safe) talked sports, cracked jokes on each other, went on explorations in the woods, and everything else together. He'd come to me to share his deepest heart's desires, and we laughed a lot. John said he thought I was amazing, and I thought he was so cute with his dark wavy black hair that he constantly brushed. (For some reason, we loved our men consistently brushing their hair and wearing wave caps in the 2000s.) However, even with our chemistry and connections, I was in the friend zone.

I was the one John reached out to for pointers on how to get another girl to like him and to confide in about his relationship problems. I was the homie, the friend. That was, of course, until he wanted something sexually that his girl wouldn't give him. And for some reason, I was satisfied with this situation. I was the best friend who provided all of the support of a girlfriend but received none of the benefits of commitment. *Hmm... Why was that?*

And don't get me started on my rebelliousness! My stubbornness was real and in full effect back in the day. For example, during my 6th-grade year, my teacher, Mr. Robert Jones, had instructed us that we could not do our math in ink because we needed to present him with neat papers. He believed that math needed to be done in pencils so that mistakes could be easily erased. Well, I didn't like writing with pencils. I preferred to write with blue pens, and that's what I did. I would work my problems out on a separate sheet of paper and present a clean product in bright blue ink.

Eventually, Mr. Jones began taking five points off of every paper submitted in pen. That was fine with me. A 95% would still be an "A." However, towards the middle of the school year, he got tired of my rebellious ways and told me that he would bring my grades down ten points for work done in pen. Well, I weighed my options and told him that B's would still allow me to be on honor roll. To me, he was being unreasonable because I was meeting his desire to receive neat assignments from his students. To him, I was as stubborn as an ox. *Ah well!* I figured, *"Hey, some people love oxtails."* Needless to say, I wasn't the best student to work with, and stubbornness ran deep in my heart. I never stopped to ask why.

However, as I got older and cared more about the opinions of other Christians, my desire to be seen as a humble servant began to grow. I'd sit and think of ways to "bless" others and to blow their minds as it related to gifts and gestures that I could do on their behalf. I absolutely needed the approval of the church as it related to my kindness, and if I didn't get it, I would go into mini panics. In fact, I actually went through a season where I almost became obsessed with being the type of woman that was seen as compassionate and giving. I *needed* to serve to prove my self-worth. I *needed* their "virtuous woman" stamp of approval. But why?

What was the root of all of these issues? Why did I respond the way I did to women who tried to befriend me? Why did I seem to fall for the same type of man who didn't reciprocate my feelings? Why was it so hard for me to turn down a guy? Did I really like serving people the way I did or was I doing it to earn their love and appreciation?

In each season of my healing and maturity, I've found sober self-evaluations to be a necessary component in gaining victories. I've learned to value the art of asking the right questions and getting to the deepest roots of the answers. I've also discovered the need to go back and ask the same questions again at different stages in my life, as the answers can shift depending on where I am. I must be like a child and ask "why" every chance that I get because my wholeness is often found on the other side of my "why."

And since we're pretty much family now (or at least close associates), let's dig a little deeper into how I addressed some of the areas that have been wrong with me.

 4   WHAT'S WRONG WITH ME?

"There are a thousand hacking at the branches of evil to one who is striking at the root."
- Henry Thoreau

Woman

A sister can be seen as someone who is both ourselves and very much not ourselves - a special kind of double. - Toni Morrison

In the introduction of the book, I mentioned being involved in orgies at a young age. Even as I type this, I can remember the dark blue cloud that seemed to hover in the room on the night of my first group experience. I remember the whispered threats I was given in order to gain my commitment to secrecy, the sounds I heard on the bunk bed below me, the bed I was prohibited to go down and see during that night. I remember the chills of fear and the exhilaration of risk that formed goosebumps on my skin, coupled with the awkward sense of pride that I was being trusted with information by older girls that I looked up to. It was as if I was finally being initiated into a secret sorority that had a much different agenda than I had ever imagined. However, my thrill of being accepted suffocated the inward screams of apprehension and awkwardness that I had felt. This was the first of many uncomfortable experiences. I needed to know how events like those had lasting effects on my social development. Did they dictate my interactions with other women?

As I sought to answer some of my hard, root-gnawing questions, I continued to learn a lot about how my brain coped with my past. I realized that my lack of girlfriends wasn't because of girls being "two-faced" or "gossipy" (because in actuality I've found that men gossip as much or more than women... Yes, I said what I said!), but it was connected to the fact that, as a child, I faced a fierce dichotomy: wanting to protect myself from unwanted sexual experiences with women while also wanting to protect girls from specific adult men around me who were abusers. As a result, I made more male friends and ignored connecting with a lot of girls. In my mind, my male friends were less likely to be abused by an adult figure in my life, and I was more likely to enjoy any unsolicited sexual advances from them. I also realized that at times I distanced myself from women or was a little firmer with them because more older girls abused me than adult males. On the one hand, I grew up wanting to protect the innocent female friends of mine, and on the other hand,

I didn't trust many young women who wanted to be my friend because I assumed they could be waiting for an opportunity to take something from me. Realizing that was a major epiphany for me.

I then had to come to grips with the fact that there was a disconnect between me identifying as a woman and feeling like I belonged within the global society of women. A part of me felt like the protector of all females while another part of me felt like the victim. I loved women, but I also feared that they would hurt me, or that I wasn't "woman enough" to be accepted by them. I didn't feel feminine enough because, as a child, I didn't have many young ladies as friends, and that made me feel like I lacked the experience to make a difference in the lives of other ladies. I often compared myself to other women, wishing that I could be as "feminine" and carefree as some that I knew.

It's funny the lies that we believe about ourselves and other people. It wasn't until I was voluntold (yes, told to volunteer) to start my own female mentorship program in Chicago that I learned how I wasn't as much as an outcast as I once thought. In my work with these young, broken women on the west side of the city, I discovered that I had more to offer than I once believed and that there were foundational desires present in all humanity that connects us in more profound ways than I imagined. Not only were my initial beliefs about femininity flawed, but I *did* have something to give to the women of the world: me!

Not only that, but I was safe to be me.

Yes, I had been abused by women in the past, but by giving back to younger women and being a protector and guardian of them, I attracted a different type of energy around me. All of a sudden, my connections with other women became more pure and powerful. It was as if when I started freely loving and protecting young women, I was provided with people who did the same for me. I learned how to bask in the beauty of my own womanhood while guiding others in finding their own. As a result, not only were the chains of my past broken, but my heart became a retreat for women who had been running from their pasts as well.

Today, all of my closest friends are women, and I talk to them every day without any sense of shame, apprehension, or hurt. I love them like they are my sisters, and I've learned to give and receive affection in a way that feels nurturing to my soul. I've created my own initiation into my sorority of sisters, and it's based on transparency, respect, boundaries, and love. I'm not bound by the darkness of some secret society of women who seek to take from me and experiment with my innocence. I have a sisterhood that walks in light, love, and laughter, and I'm here for every moment of it. Not only do I have a healthy intimate circle of female friends, but I also seek out new connections with women regularly.

At times, my heart and social transformation are almost unbelievable to me. In fact, I've changed so much that one of my mentees recently told me that she has admired the way that I can connect almost instantly to other women. *What?! Who, me?! The girl who used to be nervous and apprehensive around women?!* Honey, you can't tell me that my God isn't real! **insert wild church praise dance**

Rejection

"There are two questions a man must ask himself: The first is 'Where am I going?' and the second is 'Who will go with me?' If you ever get these questions in the wrong order, you are in trouble."- Sam Keen

I remember the week I told my pastor that a friend (we'll call him Jamal) and I had been sleeping together for some months. It was one of the hardest conversations I had ever volunteered to have, but I knew I had to talk about it with my pastor to free myself from the unhealthy "friendship" I was in with Jamal, who was one of our ministry partners. I will never forget that week.

A few days after our confession, I talked with Jamal in a fast food restaurant. He told me that he had never had a connection with a woman like he had with me, that the sex was incredible, that my personality consistently intrigued him, and that I was everything that he ever prayed for in a wife... except for one detail. I wasn't attractive enough for him (talk about a knife to the heart). I remember Jamal looking me in my eyes, telling me that I was one of his best friends at the time, but as he considered a future with me, it disgusted him, that the thought of walking into a room with me, me pregnant with his child, embarrassed him.

For over a year, I couldn't shake off my heartache from that day. Instead of feeling like Jamal deserved a good ole black-girl-neck-twist and a loud cursing out (that for some reason usually starts off with "First of all"), followed by a hot pan of grits thrown in his face, I remember sitting there, feeling like a knife had punctured every layer of my heart. I kept remembering that time, and how I thought Jamal had stepped away to go to the bathroom, only to realize, twenty minutes later, that he had gotten in his car and left me in the restaurant. I stayed in that seat for fifteen more minutes, bleeding internally after his verbal stabbing. I can also still recall the pain I felt two months later when he was in an official relationship with another woman who he married that next year.

And I am still in pain. But this pain is different.

I'm not heartbroken because I miss Jamal. Instead, I hurt for the woman who still wanted to be with him after that happened to me, who desired his presence even after finding out that Jamal's relationship with his soon-to-be wife began while Jamal and I were still "together."

Why was I okay with being his side piece? Why did I want to be with him even after he hurt me?

Initially, I assumed that I missed the fantastic sex we had and thought that it was the intercourse that I didn't want to live without. However, the real answer was simple, but it wasn't easy to come by. The truth was I had an issue loving myself as much as I worked to love others. My behaviors flowed from my heart's well of rejection.

Because I felt so deeply for Jamal as a friend, and I didn't want to lose him, I thought the best way to express my adoration for him was to give him my body, the way I was taught early on. I would do anything and everything he wanted to do sexually just to keep him happy and in my life. I also stayed in our relationship because deep down I wanted to try to fill the void of intimacy that I felt in my heart. Each time we slept together and I laid in his arms afterward, I felt wanted and loved, if only for a couple of hours. That feeling of closeness became a drug to me. After that conversation at the fast food restaurant, I felt like my worst fear had become a reality. I wanted to get back together with Jamal so that I could act like it was all a dream.

I wanted so desperately to believe that I was worth more than just my body, and so I forgave him after that conversation in the restaurant. He apologized to me and talked about trying to work things out. I wanted to build a relationship with him. I was struggling with so much rejection that I wanted Jamal to affirm my worth by taking me as "his girl" and loving me despite my flaws.

I also realized that I was okay being hidden by Jamal from the general public because of those hidden years of abuse. Not only did he treat me like a "sister in Christ" in public circles, but Jamal also encouraged one of his family members to pursue me when that family member told him that he was interested in me. And I went along with all of it.

What in the world?!

I had grown up with adults and older teenagers continually telling me to keep our "relationship" private. As a result, being a side chick felt natural to me. Deep down, I actually held a twisted belief that someone could love me, have sex with me, and yet keep me a secret side piece. I mean, Jamal would literally take out other women on dates and post pictures and stuff, while coming back to me following their date. What's more startling is that I was rejected enough to accept that kind of treatment. In fact, I was understanding concerning it.

It was incredibly tough to dig deep and discover my behavioral roots as it related to my relationship with Jamal, but I'm glad that I faced the facts. Of course, I wish I could go back in time and tell the younger version of me how amazing she was even then. I wish I could let her know that she didn't need a man to validate her and that she deserved to be cherished and publicly honored (at the very least by close family and friends), but I know that she had to learn for herself.

And, boy, have I learned! I've learned to look myself in the mirror after every shower I take, flip my hair (or the hair I've purchased), and tell the beautiful brown girl in the mirror that she is gorgeous, godly, worthy, smart, and so much more. I've learned to affirm myself and praise God for the truth of His Word that lets me know that I am fearfully and wonderfully made and that it was a Perfect Prince who loved me enough to die for me (Psalm 139:14, John 3:16). On top of that, He gave me gifts even after His resurrection (Romans 11:29, 1 Peter 4:10, Ephesians 2:8, Matthew 7:11). *So, child, please!* Ain't nobody crying over a frog of a man when someone of spotless royal descent has called me beautiful and has proved my worth by sacrificing His life for me!

Ain't Nobody Submitting!

"The reason why many are still troubled, still seeking, still making little forward progress is because they haven't yet come to the end of themselves. We're still trying to give orders, and interfering with God's work within us."- A. W. Tozer

Once I was asked to take charge of something by a church leader, and when I gave my report, he had changed almost everything about my plan. He told me that he wasn't going to do things my way, but he expected me to lead the charge in the plan he had developed. I was confused and more than a little irritated. He explained his thought process, but I didn't understand, and I couldn't see why he would ask me to be the front person for a method that I thought was dumb. Yes, he was a leader, but his strategy lacked sense to me, and I did not want to be one of the faces for it. After questioning him about his decision several times, he looked me in my eyes and asked me a question that spoke to my heart: *"Why is it so difficult for you to submit to me?"*

Of course, I told him that I didn't have an issue with submitting, but there it was. Another question that I had to answer honestly within myself.

As I sought to find out more about this issue, I remembered an

AFTER THEY TOUCHED ME

old boyfriend.

This particular ex (we'll call him Trevor) had truly chased after me before we finally got together, and I was so happy that someone would put in some work to be with me. During Trevor's pursuit of me, he would pray for me, check in on me, regularly communicate his feelings, the whole nine.

Things changed when we became honest about our sexual pasts.

As it turned out, Trevor had slept with many more women than I had with men. However, despite that fact, he was disgusted by the number of men I had slept with. From that conversation on, he treated me as if I had to have sex with him since he pursued me and those other guys didn't.

One night, I remember reading my Bible and praying in Trevor's living room, while he slept in his bedroom. He woke up, came to the front room, and told me to come to bed and sleep with him. I let him know that I was spending time with God. He then rebuked me. He told me that a woman was to submit to her man and that I should go to bed with him. I remember looking at him like he was crazy, anger reaching my eyes. His anger matched mine, and he repeated himself.

"Submit!"

THE STORY OF HOW I'VE TURNED MY SEXUAL TRAUMA INTO A GLORIOUS TRIUMPH

59

And I did.

I was angry about that night for weeks afterwards. *Shoot!* For months afterwards! I remember struggling with the thought that someone I loved would use his authority against me (although the Bible says that a woman should submit to her *own* husband, not any and every man). I remember the betrayal I felt as I walked back to his room, the pain and the memories it brought with me.

You see, it wasn't the first time that someone had used their "authority" against me to take advantage of me or to get something from me that I wasn't ready to give. Because of that, I had gained an unhealthy distrust for leadership. It was the kind of doubt that led me to question every move of a leader and to have a heart that wouldn't submit to a thing unless I wholeheartedly agreed with it (which means I only followed my own feelings and never submitted at all). It was the reason why my church elder was having such an issue with me when I wouldn't just follow his plan. I didn't trust him to lead me well…to lead me to a safe place.

During this time, I also saw how I was unable to submit to God's authority. It didn't matter how much God was trying to set me up to bless me. Unless He explained His every move to me and I could understand His plan 100%, I wouldn't follow it. Looking back, I realize how much joy I missed out on by trying to get God to explain

AFTER THEY TOUCHED ME

His plans before I believed His promises. I missed out because faith has everything to do with trusting something you can't see, a path you can't understand. Living by sight kept me tied down to the present and limited my ability to create the future that I wanted to see. I had to deal with the fact that my lack of submission stemmed from a place of feeling unprotected. I needed to commit to believing that God could be trusted to lead me and that He could be trusted to protect me, even after others hurt me.

This passage in 1 Peter 3:5-6 helped me a lot:

This is how the holy women of old made themselves beautiful. They put their trust in God and accepted the authority of their husbands. For instance, Sarah obeyed her husband, Abraham, and called him her master. You are her daughters when you do what is right and do not fear what is frightening.

I embraced this passage because it spoke directly to my fear of being unprotected. Peter was showing us that we confirm our hope in God by submitting to the authority God has given others. Sarah was protected even when Abraham was acting a fool and trying to get her to pretend that she was his sister instead of his wife (Genesis 12:10-20; 20:1-18). Even when Abraham failed to cover Sarah, God dispatched his angels and sent a dream to the ruler to protect her.

THE STORY OF HOW I'VE TURNED MY SEXUAL TRAUMA INTO A GLORIOUS TRIUMPH

61

I realized that when I submit to earthly authority (even when they are flawed), I show that I trust that God is ultimately in control. My submission shows that I believe I'm a daughter of God (not a slave), and that as a Father, God is willing, able, and faithful to move heaven and earth to protect me when I need it the most.

Worth

For while we were still weak, at the right time Christ died for the ungodly. For one will scarcely die for a righteous person—though perhaps for a good person one would dare even to die— but God shows his love for us in that while we were still sinners, Christ died for us. - Romans 5:6-8

After doing my best to recommit to God in college, I found myself trying to go out of my way to serve and be present for people that I cared for and looked up to. I would do larger favors like driving across the country to help a friend's friend get to a singing competition audition or giving someone hundreds of dollars when they needed or wanted it. I also created and planned intricate movies and events for birthday parties, built free websites to support someone's brand, developed successful marketing campaigns for creatives, and more. On a smaller scale, I learned to love sports or events that someone else enjoyed, stayed up late to talk with people just because they were bored, and went out on dates with people I had little interest in. The list went on and on. I was known, in some circles, as an extreme servant. However, when I began to dig deep into why I felt the need to serve so hard and to be so generous, many times I came to a core belief of feeling unworthy of love and acceptance.

This was especially true in romantic relationships. I felt so unclean and like such a whore for my struggles that I tried to make up for it by being as kind, loving, and giving as possible. I thought that, if I was talented enough and if I sacrificed myself enough for a person, then maybe, just maybe, a "good man" would love me. If I knew enough scripture and had tons of mentees who could vouch for me being a high-quality woman, then maybe a godly man would look beyond my past and cherish me the way I had always wanted to be treasured. I believed that God could look beyond my past (most of the time), but I never believed that any other human could.

I was just too messy.

This belief was reinforced with one relationship that I had with a guy (we'll call him Roberto) who had pursued me heavily for almost a year. I wasn't interested in Roberto at first because I was "in love" with some other guy who treated me like a side chick. So I ignored Roberto's initial advances. Roberto would call me, engage in quality conversations, tell me that I was beautiful, read scripture with me, fast and pray on my behalf, and so much more. He would constantly ask me to go on dates with him, but it wasn't until my grandmother passed away and he was the one who stood by my side, that I actually decided to give him a chance and start a dating relationship.

It was great at first. Roberto's jaw would drop anytime he would see me dressed up and he *loved* to wine and dine me. It was all so new to me, and I cherished it. Even my friends and family would comment about the way he couldn't take his eyes off me. He was so proud to walk into a room with me, so proud of the fact that I was his girl and that I was "beautiful, smart, and godly." I soaked up every bit of the newness of it all as we planned our future together, and he spoke about marrying me to everyone connected to us.

Then he asked about my sexual past. *Here we go again...*

Although I was trying to walk on a newer path of purity with him, I admitted my past exploits to him. I answered every question he asked with honesty and brokenness, telling him about the men I had been with. I was disgusted by my answers, but I had committed to being honest with him in order to build an authentic future together. I wanted to know that someone could know me and still love me, and I thought he would be the one. After all, he had pursued me for a year, and I had been living such a "cleaner" life with him.

He didn't see things that way.

I will never forget the look of growing sickness that swept across Roberto's face as I poured out my heart to him. It was the kind of disgusted and fearful look a person gets when they realize that they need to vomit, and they are trying to find the nearest exit.

Even though Roberto had an extensive sexual history with women, he couldn't seem to accept me and my past. In fact, he told me that he considered me a fraud, and that I was ridiculous for asking him to wait to have sex, when I had given my body to so many other men. He was offended not only by my past but by the fact that I was choosing to try to live a new way with him, rejecting all of his advances and making him wait to even kiss me until we were in a relationship. I still remember how I dropped to the ground in tears as Roberto walked out of the room, and I begged him to stay and talk to me.

Roberto ended up coming back later, but he never looked at me the same. In fact, the rest of our relationship was based on me having sex with him.

From that point on, we did whatever he wanted to do, and the sexual "beast" in me had her way. She danced for him. She performed for him. She said all of the things he wanted to hear. All the while, the "beautiful, smart, godly" girl that he had once pursued was muted and put away. Pleasing one another physically became the basis of our relationship, but I never saw him look at me the way he did while pursuing me. My innocence was gone in his eyes, and his disrespect for me was evident in the way he treated me and the way his public boasting ceased.

I also remember a time in college when I finally made some amazing girlfriends for the first time. They were truly my sisters, and we would do almost everything together. There wasn't really anything that I wouldn't have done for those ladies, and I believed that there wasn't anything that they wouldn't have done for me as well. At that point, it was the first time that I was a part of a sisterhood where we laughed, talked, worshipped, traveled, sang, and just did overall life together. It was beautiful, and anyone looking in saw the loveliness of it as well.

Unfortunately, it didn't stay that way.

You see, I was a praise and worship leader on my Christian campus at the time, but there were very few people who knew about my past molestations and my struggles with sexual immorality. In fact, my best friend Jasmine was one of the very few female friends that I had told. I was still walking in shame and dealing with trust issues.

But eventually, the bomb dropped with the group of girls I loved like sisters.

Someone in our "sisterhood" found out about my shadow life of sex and dating, and our friendship was broken. To them, I was a liar, and I could honestly understand why they saw me that way. I just desperately wanted them to also see something other than my sin and struggles.

And yet again, it didn't happen that way.

They continued to grow and flourish together, but I was noticeably pushed away, even after we had conversations to reconcile. As of today, one of them has come back around, and we have a distant relationship, but definitely nowhere near what it used to be or anywhere close to where I hoped we'd be in time. Not at all.

But Jasmine was there through it all.

In recent years, I began to wonder why Jasmine stood by me even while I was a mess. I had so many walls up that made me a poor friend in many ways. I was also living a duplicitous life. Looking back, I know that seeing me hurt myself and others had to have broken her heart as well. In addition, some of my behaviors that I used to protect myself often cut her.

I asked Jasmine why she stayed and she told me she learned to deal with the pains that I caused her because she recognized that I was walking around with a larger, open wound. She could easily mend the little cuts that I gave her, but she felt God had called her to be by my side as I was in need of master surgery.

I will forever love her for that. Everyone isn't called to such friendship, but we must treasure those who are.

It took me a while to accept Jasmine's answer and to get over the feeling of being less than or unworthy of quality relationships, but I have come a mighty long way. I've grown in becoming aware of when I'm doing something to earn someone's affections and when I'm going above and beyond simply because I choose to sincerely serve. I've become content with knowing that everyone cannot handle my past, understand my present, or carry me into my future. I'm comfortable knowing that Christ's sacrifice still covers my sin, and the Holy Spirit makes ways for me to create a stronger tomorrow. As I look back, I am humbled to see the ways that Jasmine and the Holy Spirit have taught me that true love isn't predicated on what I do.

Love is given to me because *I am*.

I am accepted apart from my works. I am cherished outside of my services. And, today, I am worthy of believing that God's promises are true for me. Although it may be hard for some people to accept me because of my past, the right people love me into my purpose, and my living God guides me into my future.

I am more God-aware than ever, and because of that, I walk in greater alignment with my intentions and behaviors.

Tribe

"What should young people do with their lives today? Many things, obviously. But the most daring thing is to create stable communities in which the terrible disease of loneliness can be cured."

- Kurt Vonnegut

5 COMMITTED TO COMMUNITY

*"If you want to go fast, go alone.
If you want to go far, go with others."*
- African Proverb

So… I pretty much dislike all singles ministries and conferences. I know, I know. I'm not supposed to say that, but sometimes I really feel like if one more person tries to help me find or prepare for a husband, I'm going to puke… on them. Three times. One for the Father, one for the Son, and the Holy Spirit. Ha! I mean, I get it. God *did* design the structure of family before He instituted church, but *sheesh*! Most of those conferences and events are filled with single women who are desperate, heartbroken, or just confused, and many times they leave just as broken, but with the hope that they're actually ready to have a life partner. I'm sick of it.

And I'm sick of hearing Genesis 2:18 used as a verse for marriage: *"And the LORD God said, "It is not good for the man to be alone. I will make a helper suitable for him."*

Apparently, that verse means that every single man is out of the will of God, and every woman has been born to be a wife, even though there are more women than men on the earth. *rolls eyes* I suppose that means that God wants us to be polygamous? Maybe God wants Christian singles to compete in a Hunger Games type of virtuous woman/honorable man battle where only the "most godly" survive? *Uhh... I think not!*

Have we ever just considered that maybe God created us to live and thrive in diverse communities, even outside of marriage? That perhaps it really isn't good for us to be without friends? Jesus had a tribe comprised of twelve disciples, Mary, Martha, and others. He wasn't married, but He lived a perfect life that pleased God... a life full of community. I believe that even though He was entirely God, He understood that He was also fully man and that it was not good for the human side of Him to be alone.

Even Jesus was created for community.

Friends and godly tribes (communities, churches, clans, troops, spirit animal groups...whatever you want to call it) were created by God to help us to become stronger, healthier, whole individuals. There is no maintained victory without drawing upon the strength of other people. There is no true sharpening that takes place without the friction provided by diversity. There is no large vision fulfilled

AFTER THEY TOUCHED ME

without the multiplicity of hands on the plow.

We grow. We thrive. *Together.*

As messed up and dirty and broken as all of us are, we are made for each other. We are made to live in harmony with one another to multiply the works of God here on earth and to have dominion together. We were fashioned to be strong in certain areas and to be an asset to those connected to us. We were also formed to be weak in other areas and to need the strength of our community to cover us in those places. God's creation of Adam and Eve was, on some level, a declaration that community is not complete until it is diverse.

Woman isn't the weaker vessel the way we often mean it when we say it. She's a *different* vessel and the only one that can birth a man that will be physically stronger than her. Old people aren't feeble. They have the wealthiest minds, ripe with wisdom, and the youth need that knowledge so that they can be most effective in the application of their youthful strength. We need each other. We are the ones we are waiting on to change the world, and we must do it together.

Two are better than one, because they have a good reward for their toil. For if they fall, one will lift up his fellow. But woe to him who is alone when he falls and has not another to lift him up! Again, if two lie together, they keep warm, but how can one keep warm alone? And though a man might prevail against one who is alone, two will withstand him—a threefold cord is not quickly broken." (Ecclesiastes 4:9-12)

This is the very reason why I had to become committed to the building and rebuilding of my life pack to live in triumph. I needed to establish my threefold cord: God, me, and community. I was tired of being easily broken, so as scared as I was of connecting (and I was most certainly afraid of being vulnerable), I was more tired of being broken *and* alone.

I had to become dedicated to figuring out how to find and function within my personal pack even if I gathered some bumps and bruises along the way. I realized that while it was members of one tribe that hurt me as a child, it would be the members of healthier collectives that God would use to restore me in my adulthood.

And I was right.

My commitment and perspective about social relationships in the various seasons have made all of the difference in how thoroughly and quickly I've progressed in my ability to see myself with a sober perspective. Even my faith in my sanctification process and my awareness of the grace God has given me for the journey has all been impacted by the community I've been a member of at any given moment. Some pieces of my community have been around for decades, like my family and some friends, while other parts have been seasonal. However, all have been used to point me to my victory, and I'm committed to living life connected to others.

In the next chapters, I'll share a little bit about some of the highlights and notable lessons I've learned while trying to figure out what it means to be an individual crafted for community.

 6 FINDING MY WAY

"Community is a sign that love is possible in a materialistic world where people so often either ignore or fight each other. It is a sign that we don't need a lot of money to be happy--in fact, the opposite."
- Jean Vanier

All Love. No Accountability

"A body of men holding themselves accountable to nobody ought not to be trusted by anybody." - Thomas Paine

In college, I encountered my first real community. For the first time, I was ready to share pieces of who I was, and I had met others who seemed ready to embrace me. My tribe in college was a Christian group of friends, but we were all very young, extremely inexperienced with the hearts of other people, and all trying to figure out life ourselves. We were all excited to be in college together, as many of us were a part of the first generation of soon-to-be university graduates in our families. However, as a unit, we were unable to really be of assistance to one another in ways that we truly needed.

We would often cry with one another, laugh, eat together, travel, and do everything else we could imagine. We were each other's sounding boards, and although we possessed knowledge beyond our years, I don't think we had the wisdom and understanding needed to complement what we knew and had been taught. We were amateur counselors trying to help one another with professional-level issues.

This community was a good starting space for me. Although we were all pretty broken and had no type of real, wise authority in our lives, I learned to open up because of them. The judgment-free zone was good for me. I knew that my people would love me regardless of what I did (for the most part). However, love without discipline often leads to sorrow and resentment. In fact, I could argue that love without any type of boundaries isn't really love at all. So, as needful as my young family was at the time, we lacked the maturity needed to bring about the victory for my next season.

Everything Isn't For Everybody

"Be 'Yourself' enough to have an opinion,
Be 'Wise' enough to recognise a difference of opinion,
Be 'Mature' enough to find a way for co-existence." - Wordions

I found my next major community in a small church in Chicago.

I'll spend more time here because this was one of the most crucial social groups for me as it contributed to some substantial growths and personal challenges and epiphanies.

On the one hand, this tribe was nothing like anything I had ever experienced and was perfect for helping me meet some of my personal goals. The people at this church actually spent time with one another outside of services and programs. The members often checked in with each other to see how they were doing in their personal lives. Many of them chose to get apartments and houses together. Like my previous group, we did almost everything together, but there was a considerable emphasis on submitting to community values and the instruction of the church elders. Preaching was contextual, and the push to mentor/disciple others was a crucial part of our lifestyle. There were community *and* authority, and I was elated to experience something so new and different.

I am so grateful for the communal style of living that I experienced. There were so many things exposed about my heart in that season, and my desperation to be a part of "something" made me willing to submit to leadership. I learned a lot there about what submission is and isn't, and I had to face the fact that if I only submitted to things when I agreed with them, then I was only truly following my own heart anyway. And, as I mentioned earlier, learning the value of submission was a major process for me.

The beauty and pain of submission were best learned when I willingly confessed to my house pastor about having a sexual relationship with Jamal (mentioned in Chapter 3). For the first time I confessed to something without being caught first, and for the first time, I was dealing with church/community discipline. It was an exceptionally beautiful process for me to go through mainly because I could've chosen just to leave the church and "live my best life" at any point in the process. Instead, I stayed, cried, begged for adjustments to the order of church discipline they had established, cried some more, rebelled, repented, and waited. It was difficult, but I learned to endure and to surrender to a new process.

Even with all of the beautiful things about this tribe, the community structure also proved to be harmful to me in some ways. Because I so desperately wanted to be a part of a family, I chose to submit to some doctrine and social norms that did not fit in with the future I believe God had for me or even some of my theological stances. Instead of speaking to my identity in Christ and unraveling the story of my past as it related to my "sexual fall" and other issues, I often felt reminded of my weakness and tendency to mess things up. Yes, scriptures were used, and I believe the intentions of the church were pure, but it just wasn't a good fit for me, and I needed to be honest with the responsibility that I had in choosing to be a part of their social circle.

All leaders aren't for all people.

I've learned that sheep knows the shepherd's voice, and the shepherd will lead his flock to the correct pasture. However, some shepherds and tribes just aren't built for us, and I believe that God used this church to teach me that I needed to trust Him first. I had idolized that Christian community and put their voices at an equal ranking of the God I had known since I was a child. In an effort to grow in submission and trust, I had misinterpreted the priority of Christian fellowship. God's intention was never for me to trust in a group of people to bring me wholeness: He wanted me to understand that, if I wanted true healing and community, I'd have to start, continue, and end with Him as the center. He would just use people in the process.

As I look back, I realize that I stayed in this tribe because my heart had been rooted in rejection. I was trying to earn my place and badge of Christendom with this community, and I figured that if I worked hard enough, brought enough verses to the leadership, served enough within the local community, and jumped through all the hoops of submission that I'd finally be seen as saved and sincere. The issue was that my sexual sin was just a symptom, and the community wasn't equipped to even see the root of my issues and help me stop the disease.

After a few years, I left that particular church. However, I remain committed to some of the members in that fellowship. Some of the most amazing people that I ever met came from that body of Believers, and even though we have varying beliefs about doctrine and the workings of the Holy Spirit, a few of us still seek each other's counsel on many things. I have continually pulled on them, wanting to glean more nuggets of wisdom from their approach of scripture and their discipleship models. Many of them have also turned to me for spiritual insight. God has used me to minister to some individuals within that tribe to shine a light on the power and gifts of the Holy Spirit in a way that isn't always taught in that circle.

Together we still create a beautiful mosaic of God's character. In my fellowship with them, I can respect them because I have realized that although we are different, we are parts of the same body.

7 GETTING IT "RIGHT"

"The only people that can ruin a relationship or make that relationship work are the two people in it."
- Rob Liano

While I sought to build a healthier tribe, I had to remain aware of my past defaults. I knew that God didn't want me to heal alone. Yet, in the past, when I sought out others, I often tried to earn their approval. I often responded from a place of rejection or attempted to manipulate others. I let men objectify my body. I felt resentment towards leadership. The list of weaknesses went on. But in this process, I also had to embrace my strengths. I was an artist who was dedicated to loving her community, who could effectively communicate her opinions, who offered sincere worship to God, and who sensitively discerned the needs of others. By acknowledging and continually exploring both my strengths and weaknesses, I figured that could choose a tribe from a more sober-minded place than I had in the past. Instead of looking for a social group from a place of lack, I was more objective in my pursuit of my life partners.

Through my acceptance of both sides of my character, I was able to embrace the strengths and weaknesses of the members in my healthier, holistic community.

Let's talk about how I've structured the tribe that works for me.

Top-Level Leadership

"The greatest leader is not necessarily the one who does the greatest things. He is the one that gets the people to do the greatest things."
– Ronald Reagan

I realized that, if I wanted to be a great leader, then I had to submit to those who were more experienced and learned. I needed a level of leadership that I could trust and learn from, and people who knew how to lead me specifically. To start, I noticed that the leaders I respected the most knew what it felt like to have to submit because they were also followers in at least one area of their lives. They sometimes had to follow when they weren't in total agreement or didn't completely understand the situation. As a result of these experiences, they were empathetic when they requested the same type of submission from their followers. I found myself in awe of the power of servant leadership. It reminded me that even Jesus submitted to His Father, and He honored earthly authority as much as possible. If I wanted to be like Him, I had to find the right leadership to follow.

For me, the most effective leaders have been those who operate in prophecy fueled by deep love and compassion. First Corinthians 14:1 says that we should pursue love and earnestly desire the spiritual gifts, especially prophecy. At first, I didn't understand why Paul devoted so many chapters in Corinthians to laying out the spiritual gifts and love, only to wrap it all up by saying that we should love and want to prophesy. I didn't grasp the power of it all until I encountered leaders who could give me a word of knowledge about my past and ignite my future by speaking to my identity with love.

You see, there's one thing to receive counseling (which I think is excellent). It's an entirely different thing to have a counselor who receives intel from the Holy Spirit. The former bases their evaluation off of the tested theories of men and maybe some scripture. The latter bases their assessment off of the Bible and specifics that God says about you in Heaven. In order to reach true deliverance, I believe I needed to incorporate the latter. I needed the prophetic voice to come to me and speak the identity Christ had spoken over me when He created me. I needed the true prophetic voice to be able to call out the roots of my issues, beyond the symptoms I was displaying.

My previous counselors would ask great questions that helped to take. My prophetic leaders, on the other hand, would dig up memories in the Spirit that I had long forgotten, call them out, remind me of who I was, and then be able to tell me the plan that the Holy Spirit had for my future. That made all of the difference!

I'll never forget the time that Apostle Matthew Stevenson III first spoke to me. He called me from a crowd, told me of the beautiful things God had created me to do, rebuked me for not walking in them, got to the heart of family issues that I didn't even realize I had harbored in my heart (although my close friends had apparently seen it for years), and then declared victory and blessings over my life. My world changed in just one moment. Prior to those words, I was broken, hurting, confused, and depressed. I remember how dark my life was at that time, how hopeless it seemed to keep trying to live for God. On top of that, I was technically homeless. On that same day he spoke to me, my car was packed to move back South from Chicago to live with my mom. However, in just three minutes I was revived, found hope and joy again, decided to trust God with my living situation (which was worked out that day), and reclaimed my purpose in the midst of a tough season. I haven't been the same since.

While some previous leaders had offered Bible studies and church discipline to try to assist me, many of them couldn't hear what God was uniquely saying about me. As I now recognize the difference in approaches, it has been essential for me to find leadership that isn't afraid to challenge and rebuke me but also points me to my specific future and purpose. I've realized that some leadership didn't work for me in the past just because we weren't the most effective fit for one another.

I appreciate my current top-level leadership, and because they're strong and prophetic, I don't need them to have one-on-ones with me so much. This type of leadership, especially within the church context, speaks the language of my future naturally. They can talk to a crowd, and I can feel like it was JUST for me. That's the beauty of being in the right tribe. You're built for your leader, and the leader is built for you.

Mentorship

"My mentor said, 'Let's go do it,' not 'You go do it.' How powerful when someone says, 'Let's!'" — Jim Rohn

For discipleship in sexual purity, my mentors have been one of the chief pieces of my social circle. They are more hands-on and personally involved in my life than my top-level leadership, and they give me guidance to help me to experience the day-to-day victories.

One of my mentors, a woman who had overcome sexual addiction (we'll call her Tatiana), practically transformed my life in one simple meeting. Tatiana encouraged me to think about the times when I had felt like my sexual urges were unbearable and when I tended to give in to them. As I walked through those events, she revealed a pattern that I hadn't noticed and gave me some life-altering advice.

Based on what I said to Tatiana, she told me that I would probably experience a short stint of strong sexual urges in a couple of weeks, but that I should not allow myself to be convinced that I wasn't free from lust. Instead, she told me to wait about four days once my urges became intolerable. Why? Because to her, it seemed as if I would probably be ovulating at that point, my body naturally preparing itself to make babies. She told me that if I would wait a few days, I'd probably notice the uncontrollable sexual urges would die down to the average, more controllable desires.

What?! Mind. Blown!

It was such a profound moment for me. For the most part, I was always ready for sexual intimacy (the old folks would say I was "hot in the pants"), but there were times when the desire seemed insatiable. At the time of my conversation with Tatiana, it had been some time since I had gone a month without giving in to some type of sexual temptation (either by myself or with others). I'd always go through this phase of having an overwhelming feeling to have sex. I'd literally wake up physically ready for sex and would just think that something was wrong with me. After about three days of struggling, I'd usually give in, and about the next day or so, I'd be back to my normal, more controllable sexual appetite. This is why what Tatiana revealed to me really rocked my world! I wasn't dealing with a dominant lustful spirit as a result of my sexual abuse. I had been delivered from that. What I was dealing with was biology!

Now, when I get that feeling for "sexual healing," I check my calendar, start counting down for about four days, and call my girls to let them know to pray that I don't pounce on somebody's grown, no-good son (because the promise of good sex will tempt you to call on men that you *know* aren't any good for you...lawd knows). And you want to know something? This strategy hasn't failed me yet! Typically, I struggle like a mad woman with my sexual urges for a few days (and I tend to be a bit more irritable than usual since I'm literally in a continual full-fledged fight to exhibit self-control), but by day four or five, I wake up, feeling peace and strength.

Mentors like Tatiana have helped me to develop plans to walk out my deliverance daily.

Apostle Matthew Stevenson often says that you can't disciple a demon (the Pentecostal saint in me shouts wildly at this), and I've added that you can't walk in deliverance without discipleship (the Reformed in me gently claps with this part). It doesn't matter if we've cleaned a mind out if we don't fill it with the right things. On the flip side, if we try to load an already cluttered mind with things of the Lord, that doesn't work either. There's no space! I have come to realize that while top leadership is built for my overall deliverance and general guidance, it is also important to have the type of discipling mentorship that helps me to walk in the new life that I've committed to.

My mentors are more hands-on, but they're not my friends. They're my pastors, in a sense. They're good shepherds that lovingly show me how to use the new tools that my top leadership gives me. Some of my mentors are businessmen and women, some are creatives, some are stay-at-home mothers. They don't necessarily have the title of "pastor," but they're committed to the Matthew 28:19 call to "go and make disciples," merely because they are Christians.

That's the beauty of discipleship and hands-on mentorship. Your leaders walk out your broken life with you and show you how to use the tools God has given you to be victorious.

Friends

"You and Me, Us Never Part, Makidada" - *The Color Purple*

Oh, how I love my friends! Out of all of the roles that tribe members play in my life, I think the friends get the messiest with me because authentic, godly friends are committed to my success, deal with my issues almost daily, and serve as accountability agents when I call and let them know I'm about to lose my whole mind. Some of them are the ones who were there for me when I'd secretly twerk and now are there for me as I lead in the church! They're the closest, so they get it *all*. That's why I've learned to be a little picky with these covenant partners.

For a long time I threw around the title "friends," "sisters," and "brothers" loosely, but just recently I had to start redefining some of my relationships because of my failure in this area. To me, friends have general characteristics of my top leadership and mentors, but they're more on my life level. We have the mutual desire and capability to push and fight with each other into our future. They can't have the desire without the capability or the capability without the desire. Both are necessary.

Over the years, I've been fortunate enough to have girlfriends who have been patient with my issues and yet are capable of getting in the mud with me without helping me stay there. My girlfriends have been equipped to handle my journey in a way that propels me to my future. When they make the decision to pray for me, especially together, then I know that something is about to change in my life. Honey, even if I don't want it to change, it changes! They laugh with me, fast with me, pray with me, party with me, and just do life with me in general. They're the ones that I can let my hair down with, but they're also the ones that will put that thing back in a silk bonnet and tell me to go to sleep if I go too far!

My male friends are equally important, and I'm so glad that I'm in a space where I have many of them. My male friends are able to laugh and joke around with me too, but they often remind me of my worth in a way that I don't think my girlfriends can. When my male friends speak to my identity and tell me to wait on a man that will value me, it activates a patience in me that I think only a man can. They're my protectors on a whole different level.

They treat me like a princess but help to train me not to be spoiled. They let me vent but put boundaries on me from allowing my emotions to lead me too far. They interrogate me when they think I could be objectifying myself or trying to manipulate a situation with another man. They let me know which men are serious about pursuing me and which ones are playing games. They're knowledgeable about scripture but practical in their approach. And overall our friendships have taught me that I can have intimacy without sex or inappropriate intentions. It is for that reason that I wish the church institution would stop acting like men and women should be separated until marriage (but that's a whole different tangent that you can book me to talk about at your next event, ha!). *insert shameless plug here*

Mentees

Do not train a child to learn by force or harshness; but direct them to it by what amuses their minds, so that you may be better able to discover with accuracy the peculiar bent of the genius of each. -Plato

While I am thoroughly poured into by my top leadership, disciplers, and friends, I've found that mentoring brings things full circle for me. I've been in youth work for over a decade, and it has legitimately changed my life. In Chicago, I was privileged enough to work with over two hundred young women and men and to mentor at least twenty of them intimately. I have even been fortunate enough to develop some national and international coaching relationships with young men and women as well.

It has been through mentorship that I have been allowed to teach the lessons that I have learned, which reinforces my freedom in a new way. I can't teach what I don't first know and understand. As I have lived to pour out my victory onto other young people, I've had to study and be assured of the triumph that I talk about. I have had to be profoundly convinced and authentic, knowing that my passion is powerful and my teaching creates a long-term impact.

Because I am older (or just sometimes more spiritually experienced) than my mentees, I can see the pitfalls that come with some of their decisions. I can also call out the root of particular issues. And because I love the people that I work with, I have a desire to seek the voice of heaven so that I can have the words of knowledge necessary to reach the heart of the people I serve.

As broken as I have been and still am, I have seen mighty transformations take place in the lives and hearts of my mentees. I've had to cast out some strong spirits, but I've also had the opportunity to fill clean houses. I've seen the broken become whole. I've seen the anxious become trusting. I've seen the defeated gain victory.

I know what triumph looks like in the face of the resilient.

It is for that reason - the victory of my mentees - that I have been unable to quit on myself even on my worst days. They have kept me alive like none of my leaders. In my mind, I'm the one who needs my leaders, but my mentees need me. This makes me accountable in a completely different way.

Sexual trauma gave me my batch of bitter lemons in life, but then my leadership equipped me with water and sugar, my disciplers taught me how to make lemonade with it all, and then through mentorship, I've learned to pour out all I have so that I can share my lemonade with others. I am committed to becoming better because I have built a community in which I am needed to play my role: quenching the thirst of others, making life just a little sweeter.

Ownership

"Infuse your life with action. Don't wait for it to happen. Make it happen. Make your own future. Make your own hope. Make your own love. And whatever your beliefs, honor your creator, not by passively waiting for grace to come down from upon high, but by doing what you can to make grace happen... yourself, right now, right down here on Earth."
- Bradley Whitford

8 RESPONSIBILITY

"Most people do not really want freedom, because freedom involves responsibility, and most people are frightened of responsibility."
- Sigmund Freud

During one season, my healing process kept hitting a ceiling, and it was because of one simple reason: I didn't choose to own my life completely. I was okay with owning the results of my good decisions and accomplishments, but I seemed to always want to share my failures with others. I'd say things like, "I struggle with trusting other people because someone else hurt me;" "I don't know how to trust girls because I couldn't have them around as a child since there was a chance they'd get molested too;" "I eat unhealthy foods because we didn't have enough money to purchase healthy foods growing up." Were all of those statements factual? Well, to some degree, yes. But did that mean that I was helpless? No!

I realized that I had a problem. In my mind, every problem I had was tied to an issue in someone or something else. But if I allowed myself to continue down that path of thinking, then I was saying that my freedom was utterly out of my control. Allowing outside forces to dictate my actions meant that I was more of a robot than a human. And that was not okay with me.

I had to choose to be 100% responsible, 100% of the time. If I had sex with someone to keep them around, it wasn't because an abuser trained me to show love a certain way. It was because I still chose to believe my abuser's words. It was because I hadn't dealt with my own feelings of rejection and fear.

If I chose to have walls up with people who genuinely cared for me, it wasn't because I had to make sure that no one else could hurt me like my abuser had. It was because I decided to see life out of the lens of a victim and not a survivor. It was because I chose to believe that people could only want to hurt me. (There's that fear, again.)

Wrestling with this new thought of ownership was tough for me. Choosing to own the results of patterns that were initiated by my abusers just didn't seem right to me. If I claimed my own feelings, triggers, and emotions, I wondered if I was letting my abusers off the hook. It didn't seem fair to me to have to be responsible for the mess that they made! They should clean it up! They should apologize! And the world should give me a pass with my issues because it wasn't my mess to clean up anyway.

But then I woke up.

I had to be practical and break things down for myself. The following is a metaphor that I used to get myself together (if you have a weak stomach or you are extremely visual, I'm sorry for this):

Let's say that someone vomited on you on purpose. You would definitely be upset, and you would have the right to be. (I mean, go ahead and smack them one time. Who just ups and vomits on someone?!) However, if they chose not to help you clean up the vomit that was all over you, and you continued to walk around with vomit on yourself for hours…days…even years, then who would be at fault for you walking around smelling like hot garbage? You would be crazy to think that you had the right to expect everyone around you to deal with your stench and germs because someone else vomited on you. The only way you wouldn't be at fault for being that much of a mess was if you were a baby, toddler, or someone who was severely disabled. The expectation would be that as an adult, you wouldn't allow yourself to be dirty, even if your mess was at the hands of someone else. Being dirty for an extended amount of time should bother you.

And that's how I had to look at my issues with connecting to other people, living a double life, expressing my sexuality in negative ways, and everything else. Someone had made a mess on me, but I was responsible for making sure that I didn't continue to walk around with their vomit on me. It was my duty to find every crack and crevice where the mess had touched, to clean it out thoroughly, and then it was my job to remain clean.

Cleaning up someone else's vomit on me didn't take away the fact that it wasn't my vomit. But when I took responsibility for cleaning it up, I gave myself the ability to operate in a space clear of mayhem and debris, a functional space, full of possibilities.

With that realization, I knew that I needed to forgive and let go. Let's discuss what that process looked like for me.

9 LAYERS OF FORGIVENESS

"It's toughest to forgive ourselves. So it's probably best to start with other people. It's almost like peeling an onion. Layer by layer, forgiving others, you really do get to the point where you can forgive yourself."
- Patty Duke

Forgiving My Abusers

"To forgive is to set a prisoner free and discover the prisoner was you." - Smedes

In my journey of personal healing from sexual abuse, I have also been entrusted to work with others who have endured similar trauma. Some years ago, I found out about an incident involving youth being sexually abused by one of their leaders, and I must admit that it really triggered me. I was furious. Outraged. I couldn't believe that a young person I loved would have to travel a path similar to mine.

I went off in full mama bear mode, and my anger towards my personal abusers seemed to be rekindled as well. During that process, I remember being told that I was making people feel uncomfortable because of the high level of rage I exhibited about the situation. I'll never forget how that person looked me in the eyes and told me that God wanted me to display mercy and move past the incident. The person then said the incident wasn't "*that* bad" and that maybe I was responding with such hostility because I still hadn't dealt with my past.

I couldn't believe it!

Was I really being asked to be less angry so that others could feel better about their issues?! Hmph! They had said that to the wrong one, baby! I proudly looked that person in the eyes and said (with all of the swinging my melanin-covered neck could offer without causing whiplash) that I was showing mercy by not being physically violent, murderous, or calling the news about the offender (although authorities were notified). I said it, and I meant it! I was praying for the perpetrator, but I was *not* going to allow the pain of the victims to be overshadowed under the tent of a flawed doctrine.

Mercy. Forgiveness. I think one of the most heinous tools the Enemy has used in keeping people bound to their oppressors has been a flawed doctrine of what it means to be Christlike.

Although mercy and forgiveness are beautiful expressions of Jesus, it is vital that we don't use a demonic twist of the doctrine of grace to give way to wickedness. Yes, God is merciful and gracious, but that does not mean that sin is not sin. Yes, the Bible encourages us not to take revenge and to leave room for God's wrath, but it also says, "Whoever says to the guilty, 'You are innocent,' will be cursed by peoples and denounced by nations. But it will go well with those who convict the guilty, and rich blessing will come on them (Romans 12:19, Proverbs 24:24-25, NIV).

Jesus brought us grace, but grace and mercy do not nullify justice. The Gospel gives me room to be angry, but keeps me humbled enough by Christ's sacrifice to know that I need the same grace as others. It lets me know that sin is so ugly and filthy that the Son of God had to die as a payment for it. That means that sin should never be disregarded or covered up under "mercy and grace."

However, even though it is healthy to hate sin, I've had to learn that it is also equally important that I do not allow bitterness, unforgiveness, and pride to take root in my heart. The only fruit that they produce are spoiled ones. And I'm learning to uproot bad trees and make sure that I don't lose twice as it relates to my abuse: once to the offense and twice by the way that I handle being offended.

Accepting that God required me to offer my abusers the same forgiveness that He had given me was a hard, big pill to swallow. And I recall the day God dealt with me as it related to forgiving some of my main abusers.

As I cried and repented on my couch one day about how I had really missed the mark of integrity and purity, I felt the Spirit of God come in the room and embrace me. Peace came. And with that peace came a question.

"Which sin is the greatest, Sharona?"

I knew He wasn't asking me about blasphemy against the Holy Spirit, so I sat and thought and then told the Lord that I believed that all sins were equal. He paused. And then He asked again. *"Which sin is the greatest, Sharona?"* I knew that He was trying to go somewhere specific with his questioning. I replied with the same response, and we did this for three or four more times. (God usually does this with me when He is about to tell me something that is going to be difficult for me to take in). Finally, He drove His point home. *"Do you think that it is fair that I should offer you forgiveness for your sin and not offer forgiveness to your abuser when it weighs the same against my holiness?"*

Boom! The tears came rushing down my face.

It was at that moment that I realized the depth and breadth of God's love towards me *and* towards my abusers. I had looked at my sexual sin, anger issues, manipulative ways, and all others as minimal compared to the sins of my abuser. I had conveniently for-gotten that God wasn't using the same measuring stick. I was being compared to His stainless Son. I needed to be forgiven in order to have God's joy and peace in my life. I needed His covering... but that also meant that I had to offer the same forgiveness that I had been given.

And so I forgave.

Right there in my living room, I let go of my abusers, knowing that all of them were just as stained as I was… just as in need of Christ. And right there, I asked God to show me a few of their sto-ries and to help me to have compassion on those who had hurt me.

Compassion.

That prayer changed my life. When I went through the New Tes-tament again, I realized that many miracles of Jesus were preceded by him looking at people and then becoming overwhelmed with compassion (Matthew 9). It was His ability to see people beyond their sins that gave Him the heart posture to be a miracle worker. It was His compassion that fed the five thousand. It was His com-passion that caused Him to ask His Father to forgive those who were crucifying Him. And it was His compassion that allowed me to forgive my abusers even before I talked to one of them, which I eventually did.

Even still, I've learned that it is important to remember that, although everyone is given forgiveness through Christ, everyone does not receive reconciliation without living by the Spirit. Forgiveness is free. Reconciliation requires sacrifice. That was important for me to learn.

I can forgive someone for offending or abusing me, which gives me the freedom and peace from carrying the weight of bitterness, but I must be careful not to offer reconciliation to someone who is not ready. Just because I may forgive someone who has practiced pedophilia does *not* mean that I should now trust him or her to watch kids alone, especially if there has been no evident fruit of a repentant heart.

Forgiveness comes freely, but the reconciliation of status and relationship comes with time and true repentance from the one who has been offered amnesty. Even God doesn't give His most precious jewels or revelation to all of His children. We have to work by studying His word, renewing our minds, and growing in obedience. As His Spirit works in us to become more like Him, we are able to enter into deeper relationship with Him.

Although I have compassion and have forgiven my abusers, I am well aware, by how some of them have continued to live their lives, that I would be a fool to reconcile a full relationship with them. And I've learned that I can love someone without being a fool for them.

"Forgiving" God

"We are the offender; God is the one who has been wronged, since our sin is rebellion against Him." - Charles Swindoll

For years I harbored unresolved feelings of abandonment by God when it came to how I was affected by my sexual abuse. I never really expressed these feelings, even to myself, because I knew that God was perfect and without fault in my mind, but that didn't stop the fact that I was holding anger and resentment against Him in my heart.

I would look at other women being free to play "hard to get" or loving their bodies; I would hear sermons on the penalties of lust and sit in workshops talking about how women can't expect to be married unless they're entirely pure and whole, and I'd get mad at God in my heart. I felt that if He and society had such a high standard for what it meant to be feminine and godly, then He shouldn't have allowed my sexual appetite to be opened so early. *If He was so sovereign, then why didn't He stop my abusers or change my heart as quickly as I wanted Him to? Did He want me to be the way I was?!*

And then I was reminded of this verse:

The LORD is near to the brokenhearted and saves the crushed in spirit. (Psalm 34:18).

I had to choose to believe that God hurt over my personal abuse. In fact, I didn't even realize that it was a problem for me until I went to counseling for the first time. As I sat in one of our sessions, telling some stories of my childhood, my counselor stopped me and asked me a question that forever changed my perspective on my story. She asked, *"Why do you always have a slight smirk on your face when you tell your stories?"* I paused. The question felt odd to me, but I told her that smiling or chuckling helped me not to cry. She responded with another question. *"Do you think God smiles as you tell that story?"* My face dropped. From then on, she challenged me to aim to display the same expression of God as I told my stories. It was difficult. It was gut-wrenching. But it was necessary.

I've realized along my journey how prideful my approach to God was. Yes, God allowed things to happen to me, but it wasn't His preferred will for me. God didn't create me to be in sexual sin. He created me for His glory. However, because we're all born in sin and shapen in iniquity, the sins of others affected me (Psalm 51:5). In turn, my issues with lust had caused me to have sexual relationships with men who weren't my husband or who were in relationships with other women. Just because I wasn't publicly caught in all of those areas didn't mean that I didn't hurt innocent people. God had been patient with us all, and looking back now, I can see how God faithfully continues to use my darkest times to bring a bright light to the world. This book is just one example of that.

I'm no longer a victim. I am victorious! And *that* was God's will. No matter what happened to me as a result of my sin or others, I've received victory through the pathway that His Son and Spirit have provided for me.

What hurts me about the injustices in the world hurts God as well. He just has a broader view of the story at large. He sees the end from the beginning, and so He is patient with His judgments and the way He deals with my oppressors and with me. The pathway to triumph that God has set takes endurance, but it yields permanent results.

Now I can proclaim with Paul and say:

Praise be to the God and Father of our Lord Jesus Christ, the Father of compassion and the God of all comfort, who comforts us in all our troubles, so that we can comfort those in any trouble with the comfort we ourselves receive from God. For just as we share abundantly in the sufferings of Christ, so also our comfort abounds through Christ. (2 Corinthians 1:3-5)

Forgiving The Church

"The day we find the perfect church, it becomes imperfect the moment we join it." - Charles H. Spurgeon

In my younger adult years, I found that the church could be patient with many things, but lust and sexuality were not one of them. I would often hear people's testimonies of how God had changed them once they got saved, but rarely did I hear the church celebrate testimonies like, "Well, after ten years of being a saved whoremonger, I am walking in deliverance!" In many instances, it was as if you couldn't be saved and struggling with sexual sin at the same time. Not if you really loved God, you couldn't.

On the other hand, you could struggle with cancer for years, and the church could know that it was not God's perfect will for sickness to reign in our bodies, and they'd continue to pray and be patient. You could have diabetes as a result of gluttony, lack of exercise, and the many fish fry and soul food dinners the church asked you to cook over the years, and then they would still believe God would provide your healing. Maybe even a few of the members would help walk you through developing new healthy habits—all without rendering harsh judgments.

But those who deal with sexual misconduct!? *Nah, bruh. Go ahead and put this scarlet letter on for us.*

I saw too many times where people were relieved from ministry positions because of being caught in fornication or adultery while the ones relieving them from their positions lived blatant lifestyles of gossiping, coveting, debt, laziness, poor financial stewardship, and more. I saw it, and it angered me, and I began to resent the church institution for the hypocrisy that was so easily displayed against those that the "church" deemed "unclean" because of lust or sexuality.

I also resented the church for the way some of them so easily swept childhood sexual abuse under the rug. In my life, I've known of multiple instances where church members knew about sexual molestation going on by the hands of leaders, and yet chose to ignore it under a cloud of "grace." In some instances, church leadership would ignore the cries of multiple victims because the victims led less "credible" lives than the leaders that they were accusing. I would even hear people downplay the sexual perversion of certain leaders because of the list of "good" things that the leader had done in the community.

Never mind the hurt and turmoil the sexually abusive leader had caused to the young boys and girls and the generations that would come from them. Never mind the fact that God came for the brokenhearted and overlooked (Isaiah 61:1). Forget the fact that many times, abusive leaders choose victims whose public reputations would make them seem like liars if they ever spoke up. Disregard the *multiple* allegations and the verse about not entertaining allegations against a leader only if there is less than two or three witnesses (1 Timothy 5:9). The church angered me in this area, and they still do.

One thing that I had to recognize was that, if I was truly living for Christ, I should never be fighting the church, His Bride; I should be fighting any Spirits or wickedness that seeks to taint His Bride. This was another heavyweight revelation for me because sometimes, when fighting for justice, I would begin fighting people, instead of the rulers and spiritual forces of evil that the Bible tells us that we are to fight against (Ephesians 6:11-13). If I never aimed to get rid of the rulers of the kingdom of evil, but instead spent more time making the pawns my goal, then I would always lose.

I've learned to aim high, and in my experience, when I fight the right things, many of the people I once resented become free from certain evil strongholds as well. This means that I must fight the spirit of hypocrisy, sexual perversion, manipulation, secrecy, and so forth, knowing that even if I'm calling it out in a person or institution, my war is not against the people being used; it's against the powers of darkness. This perspective has helped me to find ways to honor the dishonorable and to still be a well of grace to those who have been used by the Enemy.

In addition, I had to realize another important truth for me to forgive fully. Contrary to much popular belief in America today, God and the church are not one and the same. The former is perfect, while the latter is filled with imperfect people and leaders. The church is still being purified, and it is because of the acknowledgement of our need of a Savior that many of us have made the decision to become members of local churches. As a result, the church is more like a spiritual hospital, and I've learned that it is *very* imperative to learn to distinguish between the patients, sanitation workers, nurses, administrators, general practitioners, specialty doctors, and so forth.

I realized that, at times, I was mad at patients or general practitioners for not being able to help me with my special case. I had to learn that I needed a "doctor" who specialized in working with people broken like me. Even still, I had to recognize that I'm primarily responsible for my relationship with Christ and that all societal groups contain broken people (especially if I'm in it). Either way, I had to really confront the pride and self-righteousness in my heart that made me feel like the church was supposed to be something it could never be. My change in perspective with the church allowed me to take control of the expectations of my heart and to remain open to the valuable aspects that the Church has to offer.

Forgiving Myself

"Be courageous enough to forgive yourself; never forget to be compassionate to yourself." - Debasish Mridha

Here is where it got real. Since the beginning of time, we humans have done a better job of seeing the weaknesses in others than in ourselves. We may have made a choice to eat the forbidden fruit, but instead of acknowledging our decision, we pointed fingers at the one who tempted us. I found it to be the same with me as I looked at the path initiated by my sexual abuse, a path that I chose to follow.

I had to own the fact that I had chosen to play the role of the woman with the brick walls and barbed wire around her heart. I had to accept the fact that although I had been abused a few times, I also had a choice to sleep with men in my teenage and adult years. It was *my* decision to send the text messages and pictures. *I* was the one who continued to manipulate my sexuality to get specific responses from men. *I* tried to earn the affection of church leaders who I put on a pedestal. And since *I* chose to do all of those things, *I* had to be real with the fact that I had been more at fault than I had ever admitted.

This process has taken the longest for me to heal from, and I still practice various routines that help me to remember to walk in the forgiveness that God has given me. As I get older and continue with counseling, I have more and more memories about how I allowed my dark past to rule in my mind and body. Each time something comes up, I have to choose to forgive myself, ask for forgiveness from others, and remember that I'm a new creature in Christ. However, one of the most disheartening issues for me has been that many of the poor decisions I have made were after I decided to follow Christ. I've really had to spend time processing that.

I had to combat the doubt and the voices that told me I was never saved because I still struggled. I had to cling to the cross and the sanctification process of becoming more like Christ with the help of the Holy Spirit. I had to, and have to, remind myself that God is the author and finisher of my faith and that He has promised to complete the good work that He has begun in me (Hebrews 12:2). I had to remind myself that my sins have never scared God. He's powerful enough to cover and convert. It's His timing and my commitment to submit, that will bring about change.

I am forgiven by the only perfect Being, and if I want to be like Him, that means I must follow His lead in forgiving me. I must forgive myself.

Sexuality

"Sexuality throws no light upon love, but only through love can we learn to understand sexuality."
- Eugen Rosenstock-Huessy

10 RELEARNING INTIMACY

"Beauty provokes harassment, the law says, but it looks through men's eyes when deciding what provokes it."
- Naomi Wolf

A year before writing this book, I began a journey back into my past in a much deeper way than I had before. As I traveled back in time, I recalled more memories about being taught how to moan, perform oral sex, and to display false pleasure for my abuser's satisfaction.

And for the first time, I was disgusted.

I was disgusted because I couldn't determine if I actually enjoyed sex, or if I was taught to pretend to enjoy it. I couldn't distinguish if I actually enjoyed making noise in the bedroom, or if every time I was making noise, I was merely echoing a lesson taught by a pedophile. I remember feeling physically sick when those thoughts first hit me. There was no way to determine how I would've liked sex naturally because I learned how to have sex in an unnatural way.

For a time, the thought of having sex was sickening to me. I'd just picture different abusers or go back to the time when they taught me to do certain things. I cried a lot because I realized that I lost my ability to explore my own sexuality the way I was meant to. I'll never get that back. But I decided that I would no longer allow my abusers to own my body.

I needed a reset.

This is just one reason why celibacy has been essential for me and why learning to live pure will continue to be of importance.

I didn't want to go into a marriage bringing my abusers and past sexual experiences with me. I needed counseling to help me really think about what things I have liked and disliked in the bedroom, what things I have done out of obligation and fear, and what things I would do regardless.

It has been a difficult journey to explore my purer sexuality, but it has been helpful, and I'm sure my future husband will appreciate it. I don't want to be the type of woman who goes off on her husband or cries when he says or does something in the bedroom just because his innocent sexual action triggers an abusive experience for her. I want him to want me in every way sexually, and I want to be able to respond appropriately to his desires without being triggered or becoming the "sex slave" of my past. I want to enjoy him as my husband, not as another man in the line of abusers. I can't erase everything from my history, but I must do what I can to press reset so that my husband gets the best of me.

Finding My "No"

""No' is an entire sentence in itself. 'No' means no, and when somebody says it, you need to stop." - Amitabh Bachchan

It's one thing to know that you should say no to a temptation. To actually say no in that situation takes an entirely different set of skills. For so long, I found myself in-between the desire to say no and having the actual ability to do so. My theory is that when I was abused, I was small and powerless, and I continued to feel that way as I got older. Whenever I would get in situations that reminded me of scenarios of my past, I would act as I did as a child, giving in to the wishes and the desires of the person who I perceived as stronger and more influential than me. I believe that, for many years, even if I could physically overtake a man or a woman, my mind went back to being a little girl and responded the way I had in the past.

In my later teenage years, I realized that I could say no to a woman's advances. A young lady, a couple of years older than me, had been a close friend for years. I loved our friendship, how we were able to worship together, and how we could laugh and talk about anything. She was an amazing young woman who had gone through similar sexual traumas as I had, and eventually, the effects of both of our trauma made its way into our friendship.

It's interesting how sexual perversion works. Initially, my friend and I would share our perverted desires concerning the boys we knew. We would share specific details about our sexual exploits and give each other tips on what to do in the bedroom and so forth. Our friendship was purely heterosexual for years.

Until one day... when it wasn't.

I still cannot recall how the switch went off because I believe I've still blocked out many of my memories from back then. But I do remember things just...shifting. I remember feeling like she had a growing amount of curiosity with regards to same-sex experiences that I hadn't realized before. Instantly, I was back in my five-year-old state of emotions, feeling that fear and desperation for friendship.

I turned into the kindergarten girl who had older teenagers tell her that they wouldn't be her friend unless she performed certain sexual acts for them or unless they were allowed to watch a little boy do something to her. All of a sudden, I felt the fear of being abandoned by one of my closest friends, and that, to keep her friendship,

I had to acquiesce to her sexual curiosity. I felt as if I needed to comply with her wishes, or I'd lose one of my few female companions.

Since I never was romantically or sexually attracted to women, I had to convince myself to enjoy what I knew would most likely take place within a few days of the turn of our friendship. I remember trying to shift into that old mindset, trying to draw from the demeanor of my more tomboyish side and the guys that I grew up with. On the outside, I seemed relaxed and in control, but inwardly I remember how unnatural it felt for me, and how eager I was to just get the whole thing over with and hang with my friend.

For a few days, I tried to avoid the encounter, looking for excuses or easy roads to take to get away from what I felt were advances. But finally, the day and time came. There was nowhere for me to run anymore. Because I had acted so calm and seemed slightly curious as well, she was ready.

I was scared.

As I looked at her partially naked body and began to climb on top of her, like I was taught as a kid, I felt my stomach turn. Every painful memory from my earlier years popped up like a movie screen in my mind, but I was determined to press the stop button on the film so that I could keep my friend. I remember starting to kiss her neck and slowly drifting to my place of mental numbness (my go-to mental residence that helped me to endure a moment without actually being present). I looked at her being pleased and decided that this would be what I would have to do to have her in my life.

And then something happened.

In a moment, all thoughts cleared in my mind. It was as if every other thought and feeling was thrown from my brain and out of my ears, and only one voice remained. Thunderously, I heard the voice say, *"You don't have to do this."*

That's it. Nothing else but, "You don't have to do this." And with that one sentence, I felt a light of peace fill my heart. I felt like I had a choice for the first time, like one of my more massive chains fell off of me and crashed into the pits of someplace I no longer resided.

Just like that, a Word from the Lord changed my life. Before anything could go any further with my friend, I stopped right then and there. I got off of her, fumbled for some reason as to why I no longer wanted to move forward with our plans, and I think I eventually left the room and got on the computer. We never revisited any other moment like that, and since then, I've never been in any sexual situation with another woman. I am still hit on by women. However, I have no problem saying no and making it clear that my preference is for a man.

Looking back, I'm unsure if my childhood friend was even as curious about same-sex relationships as it seemed at the time. She always had a love for men, but just like me, she was dealing with the trauma from sexual abuse and the generational effects of family silence as it related to pedophilia. She was broken just as I was, but I praise God for her and her restoration because as far as I can tell from what I've seen on social media, she has a beautiful family and continues in ministry work. I don't think any less of her from that experience. We were both exploring ways to try to navigate our lives and numb our pain after enduring sexual trauma. We were both in the process of finding out who we were as individuals, sexual beings, and children of God.

Once I found out how to how to say no to women, it was easy to do. However, it seemed much more difficult to "find my no" with men. Earlier in life, if I had known how to do it, I probably would've turned down many of the men I slept with. However, sometimes I didn't even attempt to say no to men because I was afraid of what their response to rejection might've been. Sometimes I just gave in to the pressure, hoping that by giving in, I would be loved or least unharmed any further. In certain situations, I'd just choose to just cry alone after an unwanted sexual experience with a man. At other times I'd eat unhealthy foods, have sex with someone I actually trusted, perform some great ministry work, or find some creative outlet or work to comfort me. I created unhealthy addictions to mask the scars of my silence.

Finding my no with men has been a journey all in itself. To gain my ability to say no with conviction, I just about had to go on an Indiana Jones rescue mission for it. One of the practices that I developed was a mental practice inspired by therapy. I began to allow my mind to travel back to sexually traumatic events in my childhood, but I'd choose to relive them again as an adult. I would experience the events, cloaked in the awareness of the freedom and faith that I'd been given, and steep myself in the understanding that comes from maturity, wisdom, and consciousness. In this particular practice, I would consider what I would do differently if the same events from my childhood occurred today.

For example, if I went back to a memory where a man tried to molest me in a moving car, instead of feeling trapped, I could revisit the scenario as an adult and think of ways that I could escape now:

What if I began to sling the door open over and over while he was driving? What if I busted his window with my foot? Could either of those actions make him stop the vehicle? If so, as soon as he stopped, what would be my plan? Would I unbuckle my seat belt and run? Would I be prepared to fight? What is in my reach that I could use? I'm bigger now, so even if he's a large guy, maybe I would able to sneak attack him in a way that would buy me three seconds to try to find help.

Although this practice may be a little dark to some, it helps me to walk into my future with strength and freedom. It gives me options in a way that allows me to be in a moment without fear and prepared for anything that could possibly happen. It shows me that I have more control and power as an adult than I did as a small child.

However, I've also learned to never go through this process alone, but to always go under the guidance and protection of the Holy Spirit. Without the manifested presence of God, journeying back to traumatic moments can lead to depression, despair, anger, and so much more. However, walking this out with the Holy Spirit, drenched in prayer and worship, I've always come out clean, challenged, inspired, and joyful. When done properly, this process helps me to find the warrior in myself and usually gives me some revelation about God's goodness and protection over me. Taking His presence with me, even in the worst of memories, always redefines, redirects, and redeems even the most horrendous of sins.

I also learned to block people from my phone and social media without further explanation. As I began to create scenarios in my mind, I realized that rejecting someone's advances didn't always have to be as complicated as I imagined. *So what if they thought I was stuck up or wouldn't be cool with me anymore? So what if they told their friends I was extra spiritual, or if they told others about past escapades we had?* God still loved me, and I still had friends who cared for me with my flaws and all.

I was almost thirty years old before I blocked someone for the first time. It took almost just as long for me to learn how to decline a date offer. Oh, but I learned. I developed a block ministry where I would block guys from being able to contact me via social media, email, phone, MySpace, Black Planet, messenger pigeon, or anything else. (Ok, maybe not pigeons and I don't even know if MySpace and Black Planet are still around, but you get my point.) If I asked a guy to stop calling me late at night or to stop sending me sexual messages, and he wouldn't? Block ministry. If a guy was disrespectful to me in a certain way? Block ministry. If I was too scared to not give an aggressive man my number in public, and he began to call me? You guessed it. Block ministry.

Both my therapy practice and learning to block people from contacting me have given me a sense of control and peace.

Now, when I feel anxious or uneasy in a situation or begin to feel obligated to give time or sexual attention to someone I'm not attracted to, I take a pause. I stop right there in the moment, breathe, relax my body, and remind myself of who I am, how responsible I am capable of being, and Whose power lives inside of me. In many ways, practicing meditation has helped me to be stronger and more aware in these situations, and I definitely recommend it to others.

Practices like "finding my no," blocking people from contacting me, and meditating help me to feel like I have options. Even if my words don't hold as much power to others, I can perform actions that give my decisions weight. At the very least, my confidence is boosted when I make the intentional effort to align my activities with the values that I have set for myself and the inherent worth and dignity that I have as a human.

God has not given me the spirit of fear, but of power, love, and a sound mind, and His Spirit gives me the strength to live out the freedom I once feared (I Timothy 1:7). I've learned that it's ok to unlearn and relearn, and it's healthy for me to say no to unwanted romantic advances. I have a voice that even I need to hear more often, and upholding my standards is proof of my appreciation of the worth God has given me through His son, Jesus.

11   ADULTERY

"It's always easier to avoid temptation than to resist it."
- Randy Alcorn

As I prepare to type this portion of the book on adultery, I am grieved over the depths of darkness my heart has contained. Although I know I'm not the woman I have been in my past, I still struggle with feeling ashamed about anyone who loves and respects me reading this. I struggle with the thought that my future husband could think that I'm tainted or that my female friends will now be afraid to have me around their significant others. It's a hard thing to write about and confess, but it is necessary for the next step of triumph. You see, victory isn't victory until you blow the trumpet or raise the flag.

This is my flag.

As I was writing this book, I had a hard hit to my heart from God. An associate of mine who I've known for a while started reaching out to me more and more. Before, we might send a general "hope you're doing well" text once a month or so, but, all of a sudden, it seemed like we were communicating on a regular basis for like a week. Although our conversation was fun and pretty much harmless, my intuition (the Spirit, if you like) starting blaring loud alarms. I've learned to pause when I have those feelings now, so I did and I started asking myself and the Spirit questions. I also began to look at our situation as if I was my own worst Enemy, Satan.

The associate was a married man, and although much of our talk was about ministry, I had to look at our relationship differently. The more we spoke, the more I could see the plan of my Enemy. I was more than certain that I was a pretty-looking woman to him, and he had the mind of a computer to me (and historically I'm a sucker for nerds). I also had been going through a rough season at the time, and he was having some struggles with insecurity. Mix all of that with my strong gift of encouragement, and *boom!* We were being primed for an emotional affair, if not a physical one. Even after just a week of pretty harmless communication, I had to push the brakes.

I told him what I felt like the Spirit was warning me of and how I felt like we could both be caught up based on what he was feeling and what I was thinking at the time. As I spoke, I could hear the pain and confusion in his voice, but eventually, he admitted that I was probably right. He loves God as well, and even though our conversation seemed light, He knew enough about himself, the Enemy, and our situation to know where it could possibly lead… and that possibility was enough for both of us to halt. I'm not saying that I'll never talk to him again. In fact, I know that we'll have to work together in the future because of our jobs. But something drastic needed to be done before the worst could happen.

I share this story because I noticed that my childhood sexual abuse had diminished my view of the sanctity of marriage and dating relationships. I didn't make the connection until recently, but most of the first men who taught me sexual intimacy as a child were married men. When that fact hit me, it felt like a ton of bricks. I had always thought that my sexual abuse had led me to indulge in feeding a general lust, but I never thought about the fact that it consistently planted a seed of adultery. It was no surprise that in my younger college years, I wasn't concerned about becoming romantically involved with guys who were in relationships. I also went through a season where I struggled with setting boundaries with married men, and with men who were separated from their wives but still legally married.

I remember my friend, Jasmine, being amazed that I could have a sexual relationship with a man, be in the same room with him and his girlfriend, and show no sign of remorse, guilt, or anger. I also remember another one of my female friends being shocked when I confessed to her that I had been sleeping with Jamal (the ministry partner I referenced earlier). The three of us would often hang out together, and she never sensed anything from our body language or interactions. I had become a pro at being the other woman, and it started before I was even 10.

What's worse is that I thought I was learning from these romantically involved men. Since I was a child, I remember older men telling me what I needed to do to keep a man and pointing out the qualities in me that my future husband would love. I relished those moments. I thought I was getting intel as they talked about the flaws of their wives or girlfriends and gave me recommendations based on my strengths. I thought I was becoming wiser.

As I talked to God about it recently, He told me, *"Sharona, you weren't receiving tips on how to be a good wife from those men. You were learning how to be a mistress."* Ouch! Then He let me know that it was time for us to walk through another level of unlearning, relearning, and healing.

The roots went deeper than I ever considered. Not only had I been molested and trained in the art of being a mistress, but I also knew that adultery had been ever-present in my family history. As a teenager, I learned that some of the older matriarchs in our family encouraged the women to cheat when their husbands were on military deployment. It was thought that it was unreasonable to ever think that someone could ever control their sexual appetites long term.

I also remembered my first kid crush on an adult, a church leader. My friends and family used to laugh about it. It was a cute little joke to them that I "loved" this man so much. They didn't realize the lustful thoughts I had of him at night because of the abuse I had endured from others. My crush amused many, but as I look back on it now, I see that it was a missed opportunity for my family and friends. Someone should have taught me that actively crushing on a married man was a sin. Yes, the crush was far-fetched, but it should never have been seen as cute. I needed that early seed of adultery to be uprooted because one day the ability to be with married men wouldn't be so far-fetched at all.

Since God has shown this to me, I have confessed to friends and counselors, made additional apologies where necessary, and set up even higher boundaries and accountability in my life. I've had to make a spiritually-supported decree that my gift of encouragement would not be used as a tool for adultery to insecure men or men who are fatigued with the burdens of life and marriage. I've also had to become committed to breaking the cycle of adultery in my family by choosing to offer honesty to all who enter my life. On top of that, I continually go back and review what God says about the sanctity of marriage. I have to put in work to keep my belief that the sacred and holy institution of marriage needs to be protected, even if some of the first men and pastors in my life taught me otherwise.

God adores marriage. He loves it so much that He established marriage and family before He established the church. The first thing that He promoted between two humans was the intimacy found in a lifelong marital commitment centered on His goodness. There is a blessing that is found when two people come together and agree, and I'm learning how much He cherishes that union more and more each day. I'm learning not only through His Word, but also through the beautiful marriages that He has exposed me to through community. There's something about a husband that loves his wife well and a wife that thoroughly respects and trusts her husband. I've seen the power that comes to couples even when they have to work through the difficult times. God has loved the idea of marriage since the beginning of time, and I'm learning to do the same.

12   I LOVE SEX

"A woman isn't a whore for wanting pleasure. If it were unnatural, we would not be born with such drives."
— Nenia Campbell

For many women who have been abused, they either become highly sexual or almost asexual. There are those who love to work and twerk, and then there are those who want to look as clean and pure as possible. And me? Well, my sex drive has always been high, and I have always been fascinated by the way two people can connect and experiment in the bedroom (or wherever). I was the type who preferred to work and twerk in private and look "clean" in public.

For a while, I thought I was less of a woman for having the sex drive that I have. It seemed like the church believed that women weren't also sexual beings like men. But that's wrong. I'm probably ready to engage in sexual activities eighty percent of my life. I've just worked on training myself to engage in pleasures within God's structure and plan. However, I got to this point by first acknowledging that I had a sex drive that needed to be submitted, not one that shouldn't exist.

When I was trying to walk out a life of purity by ignoring my sexuality, I was losing... bad. I'd try to push all thoughts of sex and sexuality away and act like I never had them, which just let them grow and fester in the shadows until they were finally so large and powerful that they would overtake me and send me down a couple of months of giving in to every desire. Finally, I'd feel super convicted and get my life together somewhat, only for the sequence to repeat again and again. It was a horrible rotation of condemnation and self-rejection.

I began to break this cycle when I accepted the fact that I was created as a sexual creature. I started to acknowledge my desires, my triggers, and my sexual prowess in a way that honored who I was as a sexual woman. From that point, I was in the position to decide that my pleasure was sacred. I would strive only to allow my overall pleasure to be experienced in sacred places, and that was with everything. I love bread and sweets, but because my pleasure in that area is sacred, it had to be measured. I love talking, but because my pleasure in that area is sacred, I needed to use my words appropriately and learn to listen better. I love sex, but because my pleasure in that area is sacred, it needed to be put on reserve for my husband.

The change in my perspective on sexuality has allowed me to embrace the beauty and desires that I was crafted with. I've realized that there is a significant difference between being sexual and being lustful. My pleasure is sacred, and therefore my sexuality should only be displayed in sacred spaces. Anything less than that is a waste of my sexuality. But God *did* create me to be sexual. It was in His original plan that I would be full of intimate desires that would be thoroughly and consistently explored within the context of marriage. I plan on doing that to the best of my ability. However, it was not in His plan for me to use my sexuality to feed lustful desires and create idols that He would have to compete with.

I don't have to be ashamed of wanting to be physically intimate. I no longer have to punish myself for having sexual desires. I don't have to be afraid of what I used to call "the beast" inside of me. I'm perfectly fine. I just had to raise the standards of my pleasure.

I'm no longer scared. I'm sacred.

Process

Many times what we perceive as an error or failure is actually a gift. And eventually, we find that lessons learned from that discouraging experience prove to be of great worth.

- Richelle E. Goodrich

13   FASTING

"But this kind does not go out except by prayer and fasting."
- Matthew 17:21

In Mark 9:14-29, a man brings his son to Jesus for him to be healed of a spirit that caused him to be mute, triggered seizures, and would convince the son to throw himself into the fire. Although the disciples had been casting out demons and healing people on their own, the man brought his son directly to Jesus because the disciples had been unable to cast out the demon inside of him. When Jesus casts out the demon, the disciples inquire of Him and ask why they failed to perform the same task, even though they had been successful with other spirits. Jesus's answer? "This kind can come out only by prayer and fasting."

There are specific issues we have that can *only* be dealt with when we deny ourselves of food and devote our minds and bodies to prayer. This is not optional when it comes to seeking deliverance from sexual perversion and the effects of sexual trauma. It is mandatory. I haven't met one person who has overcome lust and sexual trauma who hasn't used fasting as a weapon for victory. They all testify that their healing was tied to their denial of food and desperation for deliverance and clarity. It is those who hunger and thirst for God who are filled (Matthew 5:6). You can't be hungry and thirsty if you're already full (especially if you're full of the types of cakes and pizza that I often crave... *Lawd, help me*).

In my journey, I have found it imperative to do long-term fasting. In fact, my first fast ever was a forty-day liquid fast. I know people say that you have to work up to a long-term fast, but I was so desperate at the time, that I just went all the way in. I needed it, and on the day the fast ended, I received a job offer that would change my life forever and initiated this journey towards healing. It was also another forty-plus-day fast for purity and open opportunities that I believe broke the chains of sexual addiction and has kept me celibate up to the time of my completion of this book. I have never been abstinent for this long in my life, and I honestly attribute it to developing a lifestyle of prayer and fasting.

Through self-denial, prayer, and fasting, there is an unusual clarity that is given by God to those who are focused on Him. I say this because in the story in Mark 9, the father tells Jesus that his son was possessed by a mute spirit that caused seizures. The father had labeled the spirit as mute, and he was right about that. However, the father's assessment was not complete. When Jesus casts out the spirit in verse 25, He calls the spirit deaf *and* mute. He doesn't even address the seizures.

I think there is a reason for that. Because Jesus prayed and fasted, He had a deeper insight into the reality of the situation at hand. While everyone else was focused on the seizures and the boy's lack of communication skills, Jesus called out the source of the spirit. He rightly identified what the issues in the boy were. The boy didn't have a mute spirit that caused seizures. He had a deaf and mute spirit, and the seizures were symptoms of both. Fasting reveals the source of trauma while providing tactics to triumph over it.

I've found that, as I fast with focused intentions and regular worship through song, I gain greater revelations on the roots of the fruit in my life. For instance, I thought that my major issue was with sexual sin, but that wasn't the correct name. I had deeper problems with trust and fear of rejection that needed to be dealt with. I needed completely different weapons to fight distrust than I did for lust. I needed to build an entirely different arsenal of memory verses, routines, songs, and affirmations to uproot the fear of rejection than I would have for fornication or adultery. I didn't need to sing songs or memorize verses that talked about my body being a temple of God as much as I needed to worship and read verses that spoke about me being a daughter of God and His unconditional love towards me. I needed to dig deep and precisely. I also needed to shout out of my wig a few times (ok, maybe not that part but you get it).

The slight revision in the revelation of my issues made all of the difference that was needed to find the strategies required to move forward more effectively. Fasting solidified my victories because I learned exactly what I was fighting and what tools I could use to defeat it.

I must note, however, that my revelations haven't always come during a fast. Sometimes the timing varies. The first time I did my forty-day fast, I felt like God was speaking to me the entire time. However, during many of my long-term fasts, I have felt like I wasn't receiving any spiritual results during the process. In fact, there have been times when I'd quit fasting earlier than I had committed to because I felt physically drained and had received no feeling of spiritual awakening. I figured that it didn't make sense to be exhausted both physically and spiritually, and I would eat. However, I'm thankful that I have learned to be desperate enough to endure.

In my experience, the effects of long-term fasting often come after the fast. Depending on the length of the fast, I see supernatural results for the next few weeks, months, or even years. Endurance is necessary. Patience is crucial.

The Type of Fasting That Breaks Chains

"The greatest enemy of hunger for God is not poison but apple pie. It is not the banquet of the wicked that dulls our appetite for heaven, but endless nibbling at the table of the world. It is not the X-rated video, but the prime-time dribble of triviality we drink in every night." - John Piper

I believe that liquid fasts or complete fasts are necessary for the type of triumph that is needed after sexual trauma. I know that some churches count refraining from TV or social media as fasts, but in my opinion, that's a lie. One can *consecrate* themselves by abstaining from certain things, but fasting deals with food. It deals with denying the god of my stomach. It is the practice of denying myself something that I was created to have.

My eyes weren't created for TV and social media, but my stomach was actually designed for food (1 Corinthians 6:13). Therefore, fasting from food is more powerful because I am training my body to submit to my spirit and mind, even when it has a legitimate desire for a thing. It prepares me for the necessary no that I'll have to give myself when it comes to my sexual sin and the traumatic effects of my past. If I can deny myself food to maintain and grow my relationship with God, then that makes me more like Jesus in the wilderness with Satan (Matthew 4) than Adam & Eve in the garden with the serpent (Genesis 3). The results of the two instances are drastically different: Jesus obtains life and victory while Adam & Eve experienced death and separation.

Because of this, in extreme cases of desperation, I promote liquid or complete fasts. Partial fasts just seem to give me partial results. Don't get me wrong. It's excellent to fast from sweets, processed or cooked foods, meats, and etc., and there are *many* health benefits as well. However, I've personally found that partial fasts just don't do as much for me. I'm a firm believer that if I want to "fast track" myself towards healing, self-control, and power, then I've got to live a life that includes regular fasting, prayer, and a commitment to reading the Word and worshiping with songs.

A fasting person is a freed person.

 # 14 BELIEVE AGAIN

"In justification, the word to be addressed to man is "believe" – only believe; in sanctification, the word must be 'watch, pray, and fight.'"
- J.C. Ryle

I mentioned in Chapter 1 that I've been on this ongoing journey of turning my sexual trauma into a triumph for over a decade now. Before then, I was a victim, and then a survivor. Now, I'm a healer. Each day of my life I get to mentor and "do life" with others who are overcoming various hurdles and obstacles. Honestly, I'm truly living my best life.

Even still, in each season of my life, I discover new issues in my character or behavior patterns. As I celebrate the graduation of one thing, another lesson is being taught. And I've grown to be okay with that. I'm learning to do what I can to heal as thoroughly and quickly as possible but to also be patient enough to get to certain lessons when it's time.

I can be whole and still have issues. I can be healed and still be healing. The important thing is that I never give up on the process. Although I'm not everything I was created to be, I am everything I am designed to be for this particular day. Like in Genesis 1, I'm "good," but not complete. However, the healing process isn't for the passive; it's for the purposeful. And deliverance is for the desperate.

And here's why it's essential that I'm desperate about my deliverance: all of my "little" issues are bound to grow if I don't attack them ferociously. Just like with many pedophiles, their issues didn't start with wanting to touch children. For many, their pedophilia started with unchecked thoughts- maybe a little porn here, a little porn there; one act of unfaithfulness here, and then on and on until the seed of lust grew into an uncontrollable tree that led to touching young kids. From there it leads to possible shame, personal disgust, maybe drugs and alcohol to cover up memories, lies, and maybe even suicide or being murdered by someone else who is then imprisoned. Our "little" issues have big agendas to kill, steal, and destroy our lives, legacies, and the purposes of those around us.

This is the reason why I fight to heal. I chase after counseling and consider it necessary even when I feel great. In fact, during the week of writing this chapter, my counselor told me that she didn't think that I needed to see her about my sexual trauma anymore because I am processing well on my own. I told her that I still wanted the accountability so that I can take preventative measures against any seeds taking root in the future. I understand that it'll be less efficient to wait to see her once a seed has grown into a strong tree. I've learned to be proactive about my progress even when I seem fine.

The process never ends. I am, and yet I am becoming simultaneously. Present and progressing. Good, but incomplete. And although I've learned not to be intimidated by my issues, I'm dedicated to taking the time to tackle them with strategy, consistency, honesty, and hope.

Lemonade

"If life gives you lemons, don't settle for simply making lemonade—make a glorious scene at a lemonade stand." - Elizabeth Gilbert

At this point in my life, I am trying to become more childlike. Each day that I wake up, I'm asking for the joy, hope, energy, resilience, and faith of a child. I reflect back on the days where anything was truly possible in my mind. I could travel to another place and time while playing Barbies. I could daydream for hours and write plays and draw pictures of my hopes and dreams. I would proudly declare what I knew I would become as an adult. I had no reason to fear. No reason to doubt. No history to tell me that dreaming could lead to disappointment. I was free to live with faith.

I fight to awaken that childlike part of me because, to continue to walk in victory, I must have an insurmountable level of faith. I may have been disappointed by dreaming big in the past, but I was also immature and selfish with my hopes. My desires mainly focused upon my comfort and pleasure. At best, my hopes were nearsighted and without the revelations and depth of relationship with God that I have now. And so, I must trust God enough to ask for what I want, believe that He is willing to give it to me, and live life without having backup plans "just in case" God doesn't come through.

One of the goals of sexual abuse, and any trauma really, is to get us to the point where we don't hope and dream for the best. Its end is to take us to the point where we begin our plans with pessimism, which leads to adjusting our actual desires and causing us to settle for what is comfortable or what we feel like we are worth. I've chosen not to do that.

I've chosen to believe that God will give me the best, even though I lived at my worst for so long. I have decided to accept that I am a new creature, adopted by God through Christ, and as such, my inheritance has changed. I can hold my head up high despite my sexual history, my past struggles with trust and transparency, and in spite of any other insecurities that I've struggled with as it relates to what I have to offer the world. I've chosen to trust that God will be good to me even though I still have a laundry list of heart issues that need to be washed by Him.

It is my brokenness that has become my gift to God and the world. God can take the shattered piece of me and make me a beautiful mosaic of strength and beauty that gives me the confidence to stand amongst greatness. And it is the awareness and understanding of how the Gospel overshadows my sin that I now have to draw upon and help others to overcome their problems and hope for more.

I can live and receive the abundant life that was once a fairytale to me as a child. My Prince has come, and upon His arrival, He brought peace and hope. He wore my crown of shame, defeated the effects of my sin, and took His place on His heavenly throne so that I can reign with Him as divine royalty as well. I am so grateful that I'm now in a place where I can renew my mind to trust in God's good plans for me again.

Life has been bitter at times, but with each day it is now getting better. And I choose to believe that the best is yet to come. There **IS** victory at the end of each process. I have it right now! And if I've turned one trauma into a triumph already, then surely I can do it again… even after they touched me.

Let's pray.

Dear Heavenly Father,

We thank You because You are just and mighty and powerful. You are truly sovereign, and we are happy that You are because You are also good. God, I thank You that You can take our traumas and turn them into triumphs.

And I pray for every reader of this book, that they are inspired to trust You with any trauma that they might have endured, and that You would prove to be as good to them as You have always been to me. God, give them the grace to endure. Give them the grace to face the hard things. And God, give them the grace to share their stories and to expose themselves to others so that the light may be shined in the dark places.

God, we love You. Thank you for guiding this journey that we have taken together. We know that You're faithful to change us, to help us. And we're appreciative of the fact that when You touch us, we're made whole.

We love You. We thank You.

In Jesus's name, we pray,

Amen.

Bonus

RECAP

I pray that, by reading my story, your life has been changed for the better, and that you have gained hope for your future. If you have cried, laughed, repented, gasped, or thrown the book across the room at least one time, then I figure that I have done alright and we've taken an authentic journey with one another.

If you'd like life coaching, I would love to work with you or a loved one. Feel free to visit my website sharonadrake.com and contact my team about my coaching program.

In the meantime, I want to leave you with a quick recap of the journey we have taken together along with some encouragement for you to turn your trauma into triumph as well.

Reveal What You Want To Heal

If you want to heal, you must reveal. A lot of the actions that we perform are because of subconscious thoughts that we have. It is because of this reason that we can't ignore the effects of trauma. Denial doesn't take away a disease. It only gives it space and time to grow and lead to death.

If you have read this book and realize that you have some un-resolved issues or you began to recall some repressed memories, please reach out to someone. Initially, my best friend, Jasmine, was my counselor, but later I found it helpful and necessary to seek pro-fessional counseling. Various counselors and their techniques have assisted me in facing my past and my fears and taking control of my present.

Choose Freedom

There's a reason why people bottle up their pain and emotions; it's because it's difficult to deal with trauma. However, "difficult" and "impossible" have two different definitions for a reason. Your trau-ma has a path, just as your freedom does.

I hope that you make the commitment to choose the path of freedom each day for the rest of your life. And I used the word "commitment" for a reason. Choosing freedom isn't an event that happens one time. Oh, no. It's a commitment! That means some-times you'll struggle and won't find immediate pleasure in the healthy choices that you make, but you must stay committed. It also doesn't mean that your commitment was fake if you ever make a mistake. It just may mean that you need to renew your vows with

with yourself and remind yourself why you chose your path in the first place.

Also, as you become more and more triumphant, your commitment level will need to adjust for the higher level that you're on.

Create Your Success

You get to participate in defining your goal of freedom, but remember that your progress will take a process. You will have your ups and downs, setups and setbacks, victories and defeats, but it's all a part of the process. If you've committed yourself to freedom, then even when you fall, it will be a forward fall.

However, remember that seasons change. What was a considered success in one season will not work in another. When children are young, we celebrate them going to use the potty or tying their shoes. However, during their teenage years, we don't cheer when they leave the restroom. At that point, success may be making a good grade on the ACT/SAT or getting a driver's license. Be sober-minded when setting your goals.

Even still, when walking with survivors of sexual abuse today, I often find it critical to always remember the patience God has for us. He hates the sin, but He loves us much more, and He is willing to work with us where we are to get us to the expected end that He has for us. Our sin doesn't startle God. He isn't surprised by it. It doesn't make Him give up on us.

On the contrary, Jesus draws near to the brokenhearted (Isaiah 61:1). Yes, our sin put Jesus on the cross, but He had a choice. Our sin then, to some extent, actually caused God to make a plan to be the solution that would bring us closer to Him. Sin separated us from Him, but that didn't stop Him from coming near to us.

Find Tribe

It's not good for anyone to be alone. Yes, we all need some time to ourselves, but we also need each other to survive. I encourage you to never give up on establishing a healthy community of top-level leadership, mentors, friends, counselors, and mentees. Your triumph is connected to your tribe. Because, like the African proverb says, *"If you want to go fast, go alone. If you want to go far, go with others."*

You Are Responsible

You have more control and power than you think. Not only do you have the power to reset your mind, but with the help of the Holy Spirit, you can do the impossible. Never limit your life to just a few moments. If you've been abused or hurt in a moment, choose not to let it control your life.

If your abuse started by someone holding your hand or rubbing your leg in a moment, don't let them have your hand or leg forever. Work to be free to hold other people's hands and allow yourself and your partner to enjoy your leg! Everyone who touches you isn't out to hurt you, and it is your responsibility to forgive and get the help needed so that you can take ownership of your life and body in a healthy, uninhibited way. Enjoy it.

Be Sexual!

God created us to be sexual beings, and even if someone tries to take that away from us or grow it out of context, the purpose still remains. Be sexual, but allow your sexuality to be sacred and holy like it was created to be.

Refuse to let the last person who enjoyed your purity and innocence to be the one who tried to steal it from you. Reestablish your purity and seek help on regaining the integrity of your sexuality. God designed sex for you to enjoy within the confines of marriage freely. Be ready for pleasure. Indulge.

Enjoy the Process

Your journey of turning your trauma into a triumph is a process. You'll have your ups and downs. Some days it'll be more comfortable to walk in forgiveness, and other days it won't be. Some days you'll feel like you will never fall into the pit of sexual sin. Other days you may find yourself digging the hole and jumping into it naked from a diving board. That's ok. Get back up. Find the root of your decisions, determine which roots serve you well, and make necessary adjustments when you find the ones that don't.

"For the righteous falls seven times and rises again, but the wicked stumble in times of calamity" (Proverbs 24:16). Be righteous with your failures. Get back up when you fall. Embrace the process.

SHARONA'S TEN TIPS

Turning Your Trauma into a Triumph

1. Be unapologetically honest.

2. Get to know God for yourself.

3. See a professional counselor often (even when you feel fine).

4. Use positive words to reshape your mind and recreate your worldview.

5. Get some friends who love you. Keep them.

6. Take responsibility for what you have done wrong.

7. Forgive yourself.

8. Remember that offering forgiveness to others is required. Reconciliation with them isn't.

9. Don't ignore your sexuality. Just remember that it is sacred.

10. Dream big!

MEMORY VERSES

Psalm 84:11-12

For the Lord God is a sun and shield; the Lord bestows favor and honor. No good thing does he withhold from those who walk uprightly. O Lord of hosts, blessed is the one who trusts in you!

Lamentations 3:22-23

The steadfast love of the Lord never ceases; his mercies never come to an end; they are new every morning; great is your faithfulness.

Hebrews 7:24-25

But he [Jesus] holds his priesthood permanently because he continues forever. Consequently, he is able to save to the uttermost those who draw near to God through him, since he always lives to make intercession for them.

Philippians 1:6

And I am sure of this, that he who began a good work in you will bring it to completion at the day of Jesus Christ.

Romans 5:6-8

For while we were still weak, at the right time Christ died for the ungodly. For one will scarcely die for a righteous person—though perhaps for a good person one would dare even to die— but God shows his love for us in that while we were still sinners, Christ died for us.

Ephesians 2:8-10

For by grace you have been saved through faith. And this is not your own doing; it is the gift of God, not a result of works, so that no one may boast. For we are his workmanship, created in Christ Jesus for good works, which God prepared beforehand, that we should walk in them.

Philippians 3:12-14

Not that I have already obtained this or am already perfect, but I press on to make it my own, because Christ Jesus has made me his own. Brothers, I do not consider that I have made it my own. But one thing I do: forgetting what lies behind and straining forward to what lies ahead, I press on toward the goal for the prize of the upward call of God in Christ Jesus.

2 Timothy 2:21-22

Therefore, if anyone cleanses himself from what is dishonorable, he will be a vessel for honorable use, set apart as holy, useful to the master of the house, ready for every good work. So flee youthful passions and pursue righteousness, faith, love, and peace, along with those who call on the Lord from a pure heart.

Jeremiah 31:3-4 (New Living Translation)

Long ago the Lord said to Israel: "I have loved you, my people, with an everlasting love. With unfailing love, I have drawn you to myself. I will rebuild you, my virgin Israel. You will again be happy and dance merrily with your tambourines.

Isaiah 1:18

"Come now, let's settle this," says the Lord. "Though your sins are like scarlet, I will make them as white as snow. Though they are red like crimson, I will make them as white as wool.

RECOMMENDED BOOKS

The Culture of Honor by Danny Silk

The Circle Maker by Matt Batterson

The Necessity of Prayer by Edward M. Bounds

Captivating by John and Sarah Eldridge

Loving Our Kids On Purpose by Danny Silk

Family Driven Faith by Voddie Baucham

Manhood Restored by Eric Mason

Redeeming Love by Francine Rivers

You Are A Badass: How to Stop Doubting Your Greatness and Start Living An Awesome Life by Jen Sincere (Yes, she cusses. Y'all will live.)

The 7 Habits of Highly Effective People by Stephen R. Covey

Gay Girl, Good God by Jackie Hill-Perry

The Holy Bible :)

Made in the USA
Columbia, SC
28 November 2018